FIRE AND BRAINS

Echoes of My Father

DAVID B. CRABTREE

Acknowledgments

Thanks to my wife, Cheri, love of my life, for your unfailing encouragement; for your love for my father and mother; for our incredible daughters; for your faith in me.

Thanks to Mom, for loving Dad; for loving us; and for proving it a thousand times over.

Thanks to Susan Crabtree, and Beth Boykin, for sharing the joys and sorrows; for taking such good care of each other; for your remarkable strength; for sharing a father and mother and life with me.

Thanks to Mark Boykin, for being so much more than a son-in-law to Dad and Mom; for standing strong in our storm; for being there when I could not. You are a hero to me.

Thanks to our wonderful extended family: Bob and Hazel Hoskins, Charles and Ramona Crabtree, Ray and Charlotte Carlson, Arthelene Rippy, Sharon Lindahl, and to all the cousins and their exceptional children who loved Uncle Dave and always confirmed my conviction that I grew up in a giant's house.

Thanks to all our friends who wrote letters, sent flowers, and walked with us in our sorrow. We learned the glory of friendship by watching you live it out with Dad and Mom.

Thank to those who helped us in the celebration of his life: Randy Hurst, Ed Laughlin, Dan Betzer, Dick Hardy, Brian Minich, Bob and Hazel Hoskins, Charles Crabtree, Arthelene Rippy, Doug Moore, and the outstanding staff, choir, and musicians at the Church of All Nations, Boca Raton, Florida. You helped take the pain away.

Thanks to John Beesley of Hilite Galleries for boyhood friendship, for the beautiful cover art, and for portrait artistry that captures Dad and Mom as we will always remember them. (www.hilitegallery.com)

"Thanks be to God who in Christ always leads us in triumphal procession, and through us spreads the fragrance of the knowledge of him everywhere" (2 Corinthians 2:14). All that we have... all that we are... all that we ever hope to be... we owe to You.

Contents

Foreword

I cannot recommend highly enough that you read this book about the brother with whom I cannot wait to be reunited in the presence of our Savior, penned with great care by his precious son, David Blair.

How well I remember my first meeting with David Clifford Crabtree! I owe it all to his sister, Hazel, whom I had met some months prior. Deeply interested and thinking there might possibly be a future with Hazel, I finagled an invitation to preach for her father in Bangor, Maine. After God blessed the services there, Hazel's brother David, who was pastoring in Saint John, New Brunswick, Canada, asked if I would come conduct services at his church. The Holy Spirit moved, and revival extended for nine weeks, which gave ample opportunity for getting to know David well. I can still see him, standing onstage, dark and handsome, with his powerful voice, leading worship—trombone in hand— and using that trombone at very strategic junctures!

Marrying Hazel provided a new depth to my relationship with David. We discovered mutual interests like physical exercise—sometimes to the extreme! We also shared a love for words and the Word. David excelled in ministry, a preacher among preachers. Because Hazel and I spent much of our time in ministry overseas, occasions to be with David were infrequent. Yet we bonded beyond simply being brothers-in-law. We were brothers.

His heart for missions was apparent as he constantly reached out to those who were disenfranchised and spiritually deprived. The churches David led were strong missional churches and faithful supporters of our ministry. Beyond that, on a number of occasions, he traveled overseas to serve our missionaries. His ministry to all of our Middle East/North Africa missionaries in Jordan stands out in my memory due to the war that was raging all around us. He became a favorite also at the European Conference in Spain.

In all the years I knew him, I can never recall David saying a bad word about anybody. He went through some trying times, and it would have been easy to complain and place blame, but that was not David's character. He followed the admonition to bless those whom most of us would not be willing to bless, and to commend those that most of us would not be willing to commend. Hazel and I lived, literally, with him and Dawn through some difficult days when it would have been easy to simply give up. But David's passion for ministry kept him moving forward until he came out on the bright side of victory.

I have known some good storytellers in my life, but David Crabtree was, hands down, the best I've ever known. Even in the retelling of stories, his infectious enthusiasm and boisterous laugh would enthrall us time and again.

I'm moved by the depth of love David had for his wife and children so evident in his final months. When he had enough strength, we would sit on our terrace watching the ocean and reflecting. His conversation was sometimes slow, and in an unfamiliar, weakened voice, but it was permeated with expressions of love for Dawn, Susan, David Blair, Beth, and of course, the grandchildren.

Coming out of dark days, he connected with a song by the Gatlins, *I've Done Enough Dying Today*. And so finally he has. But his legacy of optimism, hope, kindness, and a lifetime of proclaiming God's Word lives on. That gift continues, not only in his own children, but also in scores of young people he mentored over the years. These workers are thick in the harvest field now, growing and multiplying the Kingdom because of the seeds planted and carefully nurtured through the ministries of David Crabtree.

I have had no one in my life that I loved more or miss as much as my brother, David.

Bob Hoskins
Founder, One Hope
Pompano Beach, Florida

A Tribute

I met Pastor Crabtree in 1995 when he and Dawn arrived in Worcester, Massachusetts, assuming the pastorate at First Assembly of God. The church was impacted immediately in a positive way and so was I. He was bigger than life. He modeled his Christian faith in every way. Our relationship flourished as we worshiped and travelled together, spending countless hours talking about anything and everything. I knew his children before I met them. The same goes for his siblings and their children. He loved his family and enjoyed sharing their stories.

We enjoyed great times and faced tough situations together. We planned bike trips with his son, David, and men from his church in North Carolina. We laughed our way across the Outer Banks realizing that we were not anywhere close to being in shape for the trip. I suppose I did not realize the impact of our friendship during those years–I was too busy enjoying the ride. The ultimate joy, for me, came as an opportunity to join the staff of First Assembly and work for Pastor Crabtree during his last seven years in

Worcester. He always took the high road and looked for the good in people.

As he dealt with serious illness in retirement, I visited his home in Florida. Parkinson's disease was taking its toll. I particularly remember our last walk together. He reluctantly allowed me to push him in a wheelchair to a nearby park. He was not able to communicate as well as in days past but we connected as always. He touched my family, and, when we gather there are always Pastor Crabtree stories to share. I know he is with Christ today, having successfully completed his life's journey.

Pastor Crabtree modeled how one should live, and he modeled how to exit this life with grace. I look forward to that day when we meet again. What a day that will be!

Ed Laughlin

David C. Crabtree

Biography of David C. Crabtree

Born: May 22, 1932, in Saint John, New Brunswick, Canada, the first of five children born to Clifford and Helen Crabtree.

Early Life: grew up as a preacher's kid in Saint John, New Brunswick, Halifax, Nova Scotia, Hunter River, Prince Edward Island, Grand Manan Island, New Brunswick, and Bangor, Maine.

Education: graduated with a degree in Bible from Central Bible Institute and Seminary, Springfield, Missouri, May, 1954.

Married: Dawn McClure, September 18, 1954, in Kansas City, Missouri.

Children: Susan Denise Crabtree, Fresno, California. David Blair Crabtree and wife, Cheri, Greensboro, North Carolina. Elizabeth Anne Boykin and husband, Mark, Boca Raton, Florida.

Grandchildren: Ashley Jefferson, Lauren Smith, Lindsay Crabtree, Jennifer Boykin, Daniel Boykin, Susan Boykin.

Great-Grandchildren: David, Keegan, Brooklyn, and Selah Jefferson.

Ministry: 1954-1965 Associate/Preaching Pastor at Full Gospel Assembly, Saint John, New Brunswick.

1965-1974 Founding Pastor, Calvary Temple, Saint John, New Brunswick.

1974-1984 Lead Pastor, First Assembly of God, Des Moines, Iowa.

1984-1992 Sales/Management, Retirement Home of America, Palm Beach Gardens, Florida.

1992-1995 Reach the Children, Margate, Florida.

1995-2007 Lead Pastor, First Assembly of God, Worcester, Massachusetts.

2007-2014 Retirement, Boca Raton, Florida.
Died: March 24, 2014, Boca Raton, Florida.

Preface

In the days that followed my father's death, I sought a place of solitude where I might process such a monumental loss. I found that place in a tiny studio apartment tucked under the high gables of an off-season Inn on Ocracoke Island. This book was born as heavy spring rains painted the world grey.

I wrote to remember and to grieve. I wrote because final words so rarely say it all; because to say goodbye isn't nearly enough. I wrote for perspective and tried to convince myself that I was writing for friends and family, to somehow capture our shared loss and love. But now I know better – I wrote for me.

I walked the back hallway of my memory to open the rooms long closed up with passing seasons. I found stored memories as I left them, but richer somehow for Dad's passing. So I wrote, and remembered, and grieved on that little island, a place he loved so much. After four days, I reluctantly packed up and headed for home to take up my autumn life before winter falls.

Yet, I am continually drawn back down the hallway to the rooms I have so recently disturbed. I am still sifting through moments I shared with my father… and if you don't mind the dust and clutter, I'd like to share a few of those moments with you.

CHAPTER 1

Coffee

The day was not begun until Dad had his coffee, black and strong. The first sip was treasured, savored, sacramental, taken in with eyes closed and then pronounced good–sometimes great! Dad never slept late. He had to be up early to make coffee. Once coffee was in production he could move on to declare judgment on the weather, while adding a smear of jam to an English muffin.

Dad's coffee brand was constantly changing, as was his choice of coffee maker. I remember well the old battered percolator, the Melitta, Mr. Coffee, Cuisinart, French Press, and finally, the Keurig. He loved them all and considered them essential life-giving technologies. I remember the bright yellow coffee can marked "Chock Full o'Nuts." Big blue was Maxwell House – until the best part of waking up was Folgers in your cup. Gevalia delivered by mail, and then it was whole bean dark roast ground with a burr grinder, boutique coffee, and finally – Starbucks.

I introduced Dad to Starbucks. At first, he mocked my complicated order (Grande non-fat one Sweet 'n Low no foam latte), but after trying a few cups he was making a ten-mile daily trek for the little green mermaid's beans. He had been a black coffee purist, so I had to twist his arm a bit to get him to try his first Carmel Macchiato. He shook his head at the price and took a doubtful swig... and then the corners of his mouth turned up a bit, the crows feet twitched and a full grin emerged... "Ohhhh, that's pretty good isn't it, Dave?" Starbucks was suddenly on our "must do" list whenever and wherever we might meet.

My visits to his final home in Florida were punctuated with daily visits to a shop close by for a Carmel Macchiato and a half hour to enjoy it at an outside table. All too soon, we had to stop as he became increasingly homebound. For a while, I would make the Macchiato run and we would sit together in his kitchen looking out on a sun-washed patio and feeling sorry – so very, very sorry–for people who didn't like coffee.

I knew that everything was shutting down when Dad went off coffee. I was worried by his decline and flew in for forty-eight hours with Dad before leaving on an overseas trip. His Keurig showed signs of disuse. Most of the coffee I had purchased the previous November was untouched. "Hey Dad, how about a cup of coffee?" No response. "What if I run out to Starbucks?" A slight shake of his head... a whispered "no." I hated Parkinson's in that moment. I despised it like a thief. I wanted one more cup of coffee with Dad. I had to drink alone. It wasn't the same.

It's rather silly, I know, to wish for coffee in heaven–but I do. I wish for a smooth blend served strong, hot, and black–a shared morning cup with Dad on golden shores.

CHAPTER 2

Lake Lucerne

It was the kind of place that should live in every child's memory: a rustic log cabin on a New England lake sheltered by tall oaks and soft pines; just hot enough in August to make one appreciate the shade at noon, and cool enough in the evenings for a fire in a pot belly stove. It was four weeks every summer at Lake Lucerne. It was swimming, water-skiing, fishing and hiking. It was gathering firewood, skipping stones, and tanning brown in the fading summer. We got our drinking water from a crystalline spring bubbling out over moss-covered rocks. We cooked everything on a charcoal grill and couldn't get enough of toasted marshmallows. It was overnight camping with Dad on a nearby island choked with blueberries and ours alone under starlight. It was building a dock together out of scrap wood, learning to handle a boat, and playing board games with my sisters. It was the crickets cadence in the night woods, and the lonely sound of a loon on the lake at dawn. Of all the gifts I've ever received, few compare to August in the heartland of Maine on Lake Lucerne.

I don't know how Dad and Mom afforded it, but they made it happen every summer. Beginning in 1968 we spent August together at Lucerne until a chapter turned and we moved to Iowa in 1974. We enjoyed the best meals at Lucerne–the best adventures–the best times. Dad unplugged from the pastorate and Mom didn't worry about the music program. The phone didn't ring much, and there was no mail delivery. Schedules were cast aside and every day was treasured.

Dad and I would run the narrow dirt roads through birch and pine, circling back to finish by running straight off the dock into the lake–shoes and all. We didn't have friends along, and it didn't matter. We watched TV only sparingly, slept in rough-hewn bunks, swam and ran, and laughed, loved and lived. We were family. It was perfect.

When the last week of August arrived and we had to pack for home, I grieved as if I had lost a friend. While Dad was loading the last of the luggage, I would take one last walk to the dock for one last look at the lake, wishing somehow that I could take it all with me. I guess some wishes come true, because I've carried that place with me for more than forty years.

I can still smell damp pine needles after a rain. I can still hear the early morning sounds off the lake as the sun awakened the dawn–the steady rhythm of frogs and crickets–the high pitched singing of an outboard motor destined for a shady fishing hole. I have a dream of going back there someday; of renting a log cabin again, no matter what the cost. I want a week, or two, on Lucerne – now, more than ever.

Time passes too quickly. Dad is suddenly gone. The cabin was razed a few years ago and replaced with a modern lake house, all glass and carpet–a desecration. I'm a grandfather four times over now. Change keeps coming like ocean tides. Next year's calendar is full. I'm running out of margins and chances for a cool August morning and a cup of coffee under tall oaks and soft pines in that place that once held such magic...such awe. And so, I'm searching out a rustic log cabin on Lake Lucerne; an August rental. I'm going back while I can, where once we knew idyllic summers, where once we lived with only a hint that we were sharing the very best days of our lives.

Chapter 3

'67 Ford Econoline

The '67 Ford Econoline Van was idling at the curb as I scrambled over a dirty snowbank, happy to be done with another trumpet lesson. Peter was a high school senior, an excellent musician, but a slouch of a teacher. He didn't care too much if I practiced or not —and usually, it was *not*. I wasn't worried that he might tell my mother about my poor practice habits. I was fast cash.

Peter oozed apathy. His room was a disaster. He usually had to sweep debris off a chair so I would have a place to sit. Sprawled on his unmade bed, he thumbed through the first section of my *J. B. Arban's Complete Conservatory Guide for Trumpet*, and pointed to an exercise that he may or may not have assigned. "Play this," he said. I puckered up and subjected the instrument to torture. Our teacher/student collaboration lasted for about a year. Mom severed the relationship when my blatting tone showed no improvement – or maybe I let it slip that Peter was stealing his mother's cigarettes and offered me one (smoking was the kiss of death). When the lesson was over, I packed my horn, rolled up my *Arban's* and showed myself out.

Mom usually took care of transportation, but the green and white Calvary Temple van with *R3* painted on the door meant Dad was playing chauffer, and there might be an ice cream in my future.

"Hi, Dad." I said.

"Hi, Dave. How was your lesson?" He asked.

"Great." I lied.

Dad looked left, up-shifted (three on the console) and lurched into traffic – the side doors rattling in protest. A steel motor cover, about the size of an inverted bathtub, sat between driver and passenger making the heater all but irrelevant. That tub got hot! I cracked a window. Dad cleared his throat and made a memory that will stay with me forever.

He seemed to struggle for the right words. "I've been too busy lately, Dave–too distracted. I haven't taken time for you...and I just wanted you to know, Son, that you're more important to me than anything. I want to take some time with you...just you and me... let's go fishing tomorrow." It seems to me that there was a "sorry" and "love you" in there somewhere, but I can't get the words quite right. His eyes were moist.

Dad worked a lot. He was building a great church. He was busy with two radio shows. He was breaking into television. I didn't feel short-changed, but Dad felt that he owed me something more – so he woke me before first light the next morning, and we drove to the Boyd's farm at Hatfield's Point to dig worms by the chicken house. A few miles from the farm, we parked at the side of the road and tramped up an icy stream in search of speckled trout. Dad lined my wicker basket with fresh wet moss and we packed out eight keepers. Mom cooked them up that night. It was the perfect end to a perfect day.

It wasn't about the fishing. Dad spent more time getting my line out of trees and helping me clear snags than wetting his hook. I don't remember that I really loved fishing that much – I just loved Dad. The fact that this giant had apologized to me on the chance that I might feel slighted made a singular enduring point: I mattered.

I'll never forget that place (Douglas Avenue, just off Main) in a rattletrap '67 Econoline with *R3* painted on the door. Even now I turn and look whenever I see an old battered '67 passing by, or staring out through empty eyes from a rusty back lot. Dad put aside perpetual urgencies to give his son the matchless gift of time.

CHAPTER 4

He'll Grow Into It

When I was six, Dad bought bicycles for my sister and me. Susan's bike was a twenty-four inch turquoise model with a dropped crossbar. Mine was a fire-engine red CCM twenty-six inch beauty. The bike was several sizes too large for me. "He'll grow into it," Dad explained to my mother.

I couldn't reach the pedals. I have a vague memory of proudly walking my bike around the neighborhood, oblivious to how silly I looked – bike walking. Pride wouldn't allow for training wheels like the ones my father attached to my sister's bike, so I crashed a lot trying to seesaw from side to side while keeping the big bike upright. I cried and cussed a bit, limping back to the granite curbstone in front of the house to try again – and again – and again. One October afternoon, I pushed off and stayed upright. Something clicked in my center for balance control and coordination. I mastered a technique of sliding side to side across the crossbar until, over time, I wore off the red paint; until I grew legs long enough to reach the pedals from the seat; until the bike fit me. I grew into it. I guess I've never grown out of it.

When my mid-life knees began to creak under the strain of running, I returned to the bicycle. This time, I bought a bike that fit me. As I added distance, hills, and even mountains to the mix, I started looking for adventure. A friend suggested we ride the North Carolina Outer Banks over three days one January. Three friends joined the mad scheme and we rode from Kitty Hawk to Beaufort. I was hooked.

The next year, Dad joined me for the first of three bike trips we enjoyed together on that sandy spit of land between ocean and sound. He was there when I completed my first double-century. He rode seventy-eight miles that same day at seventy years of age. He was the life of the party, connecting with a dozen or so guys who rode the beach ride with me over the years. He used the ride to raise money for a Christian School. His fund raising efforts planted the idea for what has become HopeRide, an annual African endurance ride raising money to fund ministry to the poorest of the poor in Zambia.

In a way, HopeRide began fifty years ago when my father gave me something to grow into. He knew I would fall, and struggle, and cry, and even bleed a bit. He gave me a big bike and I rose to the challenge.

I think God gives us all big bikes – dreams and visions that don't fit us now. He presents us with challenges that involve a bit of sweat and tears – even a little blood. He always gives us something bigger than we are so that He can show us just how great He can be in us. I'm fifty-six years old and Dad is gone. I'm asking my heavenly Father to give me a new bike: a couple of sizes too big for me, one more dream that causes me to shudder, one more challenge that requires, like never before, that I trust Him fully for the power, passion, persistence, and love to see it through.

In 2014, HopeRide covered a thousand miles in ten days, crossing South Africa from the Atlantic to the Indian Ocean. The ride was dedicated to my father's memory. I couldn't help but think how he would have loved to ride that African plain at my side. HopeRide funds water wells, Sunday schools, education, missionary vehicles and basic necessities for children in western Zambia. When Dad gave me my first bike, he said that I would grow into it. Now I marvel at what grew out of it.

A few years ago, Dad and I took four days to trace a path that linked our favorite places from the Great Smoky Mountains to the sandy shores of the Outer Banks in North Carolina. I was shocked at his decline. His cycling days were over. As I drove he slept the sleep of old men. I realized that our grand adventures were mostly behind us. We stopped earlier than planned each night – the drive just tired him out – but he enjoyed chicken pot pie at the Applewood Barn, downed a couple bowls of chowder at Kitty Hawk, and capped it all with conch fritters at Howard's Pub on Ocracoke Island. We talked of preaching, family, riding, and running; of my boyhood and his; of living a full life and finishing strong. Sometimes we didn't talk it all. Sometimes you don't need words.

Parkinson's was increasingly evident in a vacant stare, stiff gait, wandering thoughts, increasing tremors and stumbles. Yet the miles uncovered bicycle memories that were fluid, vivid, and graceful. We relived our great moments as the mile markers whipped by, covering the roads we had covered together. I knew that I would soon have to go on without him. He knew it too. We didn't talk much about dying – we were too busy living. Now, though he is gone, when mountains loom large, I feel his hand on my shoulder, and I hear his voice, "Don't worry, Dave, you'll grow into it."

CHAPTER 5

Camping

Dad loved camping. He loved to set up our old-school, six-man, khaki-colored, heavy canvas, steel-framed, army-style wall tent. He loved hammering down vampire stakes with a clown mallet – tying back musty window flaps to air out last month's adventure. He fussed over the attachable screen kitchen, a must at mealtime when camping in the kingdom of flies. Total set up took a couple of hours after which Dad would step back to survey his ship-shape campsite before pumping up the Coleman stove and putting on the coffee.

Since his passing, I remember more and more camping stories from places once forgotten now so close as yesterday. Dad always wanted to be near the water, preferably on a point where a bit of breeze would drive away the flies. I remember our two-night foray into Shepody Woods where we fished the rapids and counted stars. I long for our summer days at Riverbend, where we rushed to get one of the choice spots on a tiny isthmus jutting out into a crystal-clear, stone-bottomed river. I want to see Pleasant Bay again (surely one of the most beautiful places in the world), nestled at the base of the mountains on the eastern shore of Cape Breton Island. I remember a late-night set up in a farmer's pasture, pitching camp in miserable rain on a rare trip with Mom, who announced with particular eloquence to all living creatures her utter hatred of camping. I remember Dad buying Atlantic salmon off a fishing boat after it tied up at a wharf at Ingonish, Cape Breton, then grilling salmon steaks over a fire pit on a stony beach.

I can still hear him rummaging around the screen kitchen in the pre-dawn and pumping up the lantern and four-burner stove until the white gas whistled. Early light cast Dad's ever-moving shadow on the front wall of the tent. I still feel the musky warmth of a sleeping bag against the dampness of the morning. I hear Dad's battered coffee pot beginning to percolate, the bacon sizzling on contact with the cast iron skillet, cracking eggs, and the rough clatter of Mom's discarded silverware on a wooden picnic table.

I remember the mad rush to pull on layers against the cold; fighting the zipper on the front tent flap that always stuck a bit when zipped shut by Dad's strong hand. I emerged to a singular sight, regardless of location: the sight of a happy man with a steaming cup of coffee in one hand, a spatula in the other, a smile, a joke, a suggestion that we might have just enjoyed the best night's sleep ever. "Sit down, Dave. How about some breakfast?" He loved that old tent, and the thousand or more memories he made there with his kids, and occasionally, Mom.

When Mom came along, the menu was expanded and she praised Dad's grilling abilities as though he were the undisputed master of charcoal (and he was). She was ever the good sport, with the exception of the pasture disaster. She saw what it meant to her children and her husband, so she put up with the mess that comes with camping and cataloged a few rich memories of her own.

When we relocated from New Brunswick to Iowa in '74, the tent didn't make the move. It went at a bargain price to a charismatic Catholic priest at our yard sale and I helped him load it into a van. I'd like to think that he enjoyed it as much as we did, but for the life of me, I can't imagine how.

CHAPTER 6

Take Me With You

In the late 1960's Dad was enjoying a rich season of growth in his ministry. His radio ministry would soon be followed by a successful television presence. Doors opened regionally and regularly with speaking opportunities. In some cases, our church sent an entire team with him. In some cases, he went alone.

Our hometown, Saint John, was located on the Bay of Fundy, a magnificent body of water separating New Brunswick from Nova Scotia. The Bay boasts tides among the highest in the world, great fishing, violent potentials, choking fog, and bitter winter cold. From the port of Saint John to the port of Digby, Nova Scotia, the ferry crossing can be made in two hours if the weather is good. To drive the same requires six to seven hours. Dad was asked to speak at some sort of rally in Digby. He lit up my world when he asked, "Dave, why don't you go with me?"

We boarded the *Princess of Acadia* and steamed out of Saint John harbor, just the two of us. There was a small galley on board and I could have anything I wanted. We wandered the ship together from stem to stern. We talked about going fishing, and how we might, someday, travel to Boston to watch the Boston Bruins play the Montreal Canadiens. We stood at the bow, like two grizzled old salts, until the cold drove us back to the warmth of the galley.

I don't remember that Dad imparted any particular wisdom as the ship plowed through the Bay. I don't remember a defining moment in our journey. I have only a vague memory of walking down a steel staircase to the car deck to disembark in Nova Scotia. I remember Dad speaking in a high school auditorium that night. I'm sure that there was some advance for the Kingdom of God owing to Dad's ministry – but the thing I remember – the thing that mattered – the bit that survives in my weathered memory: Dad asked me to go. It was just the two of us.

That trip reminds me that it's been a while since I've taken my four year-old grandsons to breakfast– just the twins and me and a short stack drowning in maple syrup. I think I'll take them to *Tex and Shirley's* and listen to them rattle on. If I get the chance, I'll tell them about crossing the Bay of Fundy on the *Princess of Acadia* with the man they called "Great Papa." There is a wish that lives in the depths of every boy's soul, a wish for time with a father, a wish that says, "Take me with you."

CHAPTER 7

The 10-Speed

Sometime around 1970, in the rising popularity of ten-speed bicycles, my buddies, John and David Beesley, got new ten-speeds from Sears. By comparison, my Eaton Glider three-speed was uncool. I don't remember how I talked Dad into a new ten-speed. He must have wanted one too. It was decided that we would share the new bike. I was ecstatic when we picked out a beautiful white ten-speed and loaded it into the back of a church van. It came with fenders, and I lobbied all the way home for their removal. Dad was riding for recreation–I was riding for adventure, and fashion. Dad wanted to get in shape–I wanted to be cool. Our shared bicycle experiment lasted about ten days.

I had joined a group of six or seven guys in the neighborhood for an evening ride. I was riding my new white steed recently stripped of fenders and looking low and racy. We cruised, we sprinted, we laughed, we taunted, climbing hills and running stop signs – invincible. I was talking to the guy on my left. I didn't see the parked car on the right. There was no warning, no brake, no bracing myself before I drilled my beautiful bike into the rear bumper of a '69 Plymouth. There is nothing cool about crashing into a parked car, even on a low and racy ten-speed.

I was bruised, not broken, more embarrassed than frightened, that is, until I looked at the bike – the shared bike – Dad's bike. The front wheel was bent like a taco. The forks were pushed back so severely that the handlebars could not turn fully. I walked home, dragging my bike and struggling to find a plausible explanation for the carnage. Dad was angry. It would have been one thing if a car had clipped me, but I hit a parked car... *a parked car!*

He let me stew for a while after admonishing me to "pay attention–slow down–stop talking so much–quit showing off." The next day, Dad went back to Sears and bought another white ten-speed with fenders and warned me not to touch it. The shattered bike was mine. The repairs were on me.

A kid down the street was able to get my wheel straightened to the point where the brakes wouldn't rub. I did odd jobs and saved my quarters until I had enough money to order new front forks from Sears. In a few weeks I was back in the pack! I had earned the fix.

That bike took me everywhere. Strangest thing though; I remember countless miles with my friend, John Beesley, but I don't think Dad and I ever took the white bikes out for a ride together. I guess he figured that riding with the guy who had plastered himself all over the back of a parked Plymouth wasn't worth the risk.

CHAPTER 8

Lac Seul

At sixteen, I passed an awkward school year having just transitioned from my native Canada to the flatlands of Iowa. It was the age of long hair, muscle cars, the Eagles and the Doobie Brothers; forbidden fruit for a Pentecostal preachers kid. Disco was yet to litter the airwaves. Computers required whole suites of rooms and punch cards preceded keyboards. I had a job as a fry cook, a steady girlfriend, oily skin, and a bad attitude. Dad had just helped me purchase my first car, a 1969 Camaro. Of all the cars I have ever owned, that Camaro is the only one I have ever wanted back, but it's probably been reduced to paper clips by now.

It was a season marked by doubt. Some of my teachers were openly hostile to Christianity. My psychology teacher took pleasure in quizzing me with ethics questions carefully honed to lead one to an agnostic point of view. He knew that I was a preacher's kid, and he singled me out for his "three people in a boat–not enough food – what would you do" questions. I resented his unwanted attention. I dreamed of putting him in a three-man boat. The decision as to who goes overboard would have been... elementary.

Dad suspected that I was drifting: but then, who can be sure in the foggy moors of the middle teens? "Dave, let's go fishing," he suggested. "I've got a friend who wants to go to Ontario after Walleye. What do you say?" I was all in. My agnostic drift had no impact on my love for Dad. I craved time with him.

We loaded our '74 T-Bird, a land yacht sporting an enormous hood and bumpers, and drove north to join the rest of the fishing party in Minneapolis. A further day's journey north put us in a cabin on a small branch leading into Lac Seul, a massive body of water covering 640 square miles of Canadian wilderness.

At first light we split our gear between a rented aluminum boat and a canoe equipped with a tiny outboard motor. Traveling in tandem, we hugged the shoreline for what seemed hours before setting up camp on a rocky point. The few fish we hooked were cooked over an open fire. We fought squadrons of mutant deer flies, slept the sleep of the deep woods, and chafed under the taxing legalism of a team member who held deep environmental convictions.

Loading out is never so orderly as loading in. Somehow, I found myself in the bow of the canoe, motoring alongside the aluminum boat where Dad occupied the same relative position. Somewhere in the middle of that inland ocean a storm blew in, or blew up, and our adventure took a dangerous twist. Waves were coming over the bows of both boats. Our carefully bagged trash was seized by a single gust, torn asunder, and cast upon the thrashing waters (so much for environmentalism). Fishing gear washed out of the canoe. Rain blew sideways. The canoe was pitching, the tiny outboard straining, and there was a moment when, looking across the churning divide, our eyes locked... Dad, and me, and primal fear. I wanted more than anything to be with him.

We struggled to the shore; shaken, swamped, and somewhat lighter for the fishing gear and non-biodegradables that bobbed in the lake. The rain abated and we repacked to finish our journey. As final preparations were made, Dad's hand fell heavy on my shoulder. His voice broke an awkward silence with unquestionable authority, "Dave rides with me", and all was right with the world. For the next two hours we sat together in the bow of the aluminum boat, quiet at first, then laughing to tears over our visibly frustrated environmentalist, mutant flies, empty coolers, and ill-conceived adventures. At some point, he threw an arm around me, leaned in close, choked up a bit and said, "Dave, I was scared that I would lose you. I will never let us be separated again–never."

But now we are – separated again. I can't see him through this storm, but he has given me what I need to make it through: a tender fatherhood, an unshakable faith, an easy laughter, and an unconditional love.

CHAPTER 9

He Hated It

I was a longhaired drummer in a college band. Dad didn't appreciate our style or volume. We didn't connect over my drums, or guitars, or taste in music. He once flipped through my records and destroyed a half dozen he found objectionable. After that ugly scene I made sure that he wouldn't find my albums objectionable (I made sure that he wouldn't find them at all).

When I installed a new stereo in my Chevy van, complete with power booster and graphic equalizer, I thought he might be impressed. I took him for a ride down Euclid Avenue and cranked up the volume on Earth, Wind, and Fire's *Spirit* album. "Isn't that great?" I asked. He later claimed that he couldn't hear the question, or anything else for a week. He gleefully told all who would listen that he promised God that if he ever got out of my van he would never get back in again. I think he kept that promise. He hated most of the music I loved so loud.

Dad had decided that long hair was not a hill to die on. I sported a massive 'fro' that Dad described as "an explosion in a shredded wheat factory." He grumbled about it between cuts, which I think came about every six months – but we never fought over hair. I would have done whatever he asked if he had elevated the issue, but he didn't. His shredded wheat metaphor was close to the truth. I looked like a hippy, and he hated it.

I've searched the seams of my memory for things about me that Dad hated, and nothing comes to mind beyond loud music and the 'fro.' I knew Dad hated these things, but I knew he didn't hate me. I was undisciplined, and he loved me anyway. I was a mess, and he loved me in my scruffiness. I was mischievous, but he didn't overreact to the infantile attitudes or asinine adventures that shadowed my slouching adolescence. I was distracted, disruptive, grubby, lazy, and girl-crazy. He was steady. I guest he never forgot what it was like to be young and struggling to find your place. We were probably never further apart than in the summer of '79 but his love for me was never in doubt, though I was, admittedly, unlovable, and in desperate need of earplugs and a haircut (now I need hair plugs and earphones).

He couldn't have believed, nor could I, that I would be assuming a pastorate just twenty months later, or that our talks would revolve around preaching and study instead of girlfriends and pizza. Yet, one Sunday night in April of '81 I was calling him with the news that Stockton Assembly of God had invited me to their pulpit. I was starting my tenure as their

Pastor, by God's amazing grace, on Easter Sunday morning.

I'm forever grateful for a Dad who knew what really mattered; who would not make a fossil out of an argument; who could hate dumb stuff and love a dumb kid... like me. Dad avoided extremes and gave everyone room to grow. A grin was always lurking nearby. The hands that disciplined were connected to arms that embraced.

In recent years I've discovered, in myself, a growing intolerance for loud noises, and hair is no longer an issue. I am conservative. I am uncool. I am my Dad, or at least I hope I am... I certainly hope to be.

CHAPTER 10

Running With Dad

Ashe County, North Carolina–Smoky Mountain morning–running an abandoned ribbon of asphalt propped up on the banks of the New River with Dad. Mist clings to the walls of mountain laurel. Coffee awaits us at a cabin, along with a thick slice of fresh homemade bread topped with butter and strawberry preserves.

Yesterday, we stopped in at the Todd General Store, a time capsule built in 1914, complete with rough plank floors and a pot bellied stove. Four old men in overalls and feed store caps sat around the fire talking about pickup trucks and good ole boys. They took a passing and dismissive notice of our tracksuits and running shoes. We weren't invited to pull up a chair. I imagine that we looked as out of place as a smart phone in a Norman Rockwell painting.

Osa Norris, a local baker, supplies the store with fresh bakery items, filling the rugged space with hunger-inducing aromas that remind men of a certain age of their grandmother's kitchens. Old tin signs cling to the rough-hewn walls – authentic in their rusty splendor. Nothing is level or tidy here. Nothing lacks for scratches, dents, or wear marks. On the same aisle you can find soap, cereal, and light bulbs. Nothing is built in or coordinated.

The front porch held three weathered rockers overlooking a crossroads and river beyond. Dad loved the place – and the pace. It's a place and pace that time forgot – and that's why we were there; to forget about schedules, appointments, budgets, hospitals, and funeral homes; to reconnect as a father and son away from the push and the pulpit – to run a few miles together – to share an empty country road, winding with the river in the stillness of the dawn.

Dad has always been a runner. He was a regular at the black cinder track below the skating rink in the Greendale subdivision where I grew up. I remember running with him as a little boy, struggling for a couple of laps before collapsing on the bleachers while Dad just kept chugging away. Sometimes I explored the baseball dugouts, or played around in the sand pit where people practiced the long jump, but mostly I rested up on the bleachers and watched him finish his circuit to fall in beside him and try for another lap. Dad was a runner–I wanted to be runner too.

Through the years Dad and I have run wherever life has taken us. We have run on cinder tracks, abandoned rail lines, country roads, and the occasional treadmill. We have run at dawn in Cheboksary, Russia. We have run hard sand beaches, and greenways, wooded trails, and river walks. We have run under the Palm trees around the PGA National Golf Course.

Now we're running Ashe County, alone, except for the sound of our footfalls and the song of the river under an October sky. We've got two more days for books and coffee, running and rocking on the broad porch of our mountain hideaway... two more days of homemade bread and strawberry preserves... two more days for old stories and new memories... two more days until the fire goes out and we have to go home. But for now life is just about as good as it gets; sharing a road, a river, and a run at dawn with Dad.

CHAPTER 11

Echoes of My Father

D ad loved everything about preaching. He cherished the printed volumes of past masters of the pulpit. He marveled at the prowess of his colleagues. He thrilled in the pursuit of the message. He relished hours spent in a quiet study. He loved language, and treated a newly discovered word as a specialty tool for life's repair. He rose to attain the rank of orator. He used humor, culture, irony, allegory, and history to set grand windows into the block and sheetrock walls of systematic theology. He tapped into every emotion, used his whole body for punctuation, burned fervently and loved gently, opened with challenge and closed with invitation.

I was traveling with him, somewhere in the northeast, when he popped a cassette into the player and said, "You've got to listen to this guy!" He had come across cassette tape recordings of Ravi Zacharias speaking at Harvard University. Those addresses, later released in print under the title, *Can Man Live Without God*, were powerful in their apologetic argument and rhetorical elegance. We rode and listened in a state of awe, uttering the occasional "wow... oh my... powerful... brilliant!" Dad loved great preaching.

I was at his side at a mass gathering in the Midwest when Dr. Harold Carter "blew up the room" with a preaching masterpiece that drew 10,000 people to their feet with a shout of praise so powerful, so pure. I've not heard anything like it this side of heaven. I'll never forget Dad's face–so alive–so happy–so thrilled.

We were once sitting in his parsonage den watching T. D. Jakes turn four simple words into a cosmic call-to-arms, and I glanced at Dad: sitting on the edge of his recliner – leaning towards the screen – lips moving without sound... and I loved my Dad in that moment. I loved his love of preaching.

He was enormously proud of his preacher brother, Charles. When I was a rookie, he sent me a package of tapes of Charles preaching at a camp meeting and said, "you've got to listen to this!" I cannibalized those tapes and preached well beyond my knowledge and experience for weeks. He considered his brother-in-law, Bob Hoskins to be a master communicator, calling him, "the most amazing man I ever met." He marveled at the pulpit prowess of my late Uncle, Don Rippy, another brother-in-law, whose sermons at the harvest time convention still live in my memory, though I was barely ten years old at their preaching. Dad was enormously proud of his former associate, Randy Hurst, whose unique style and gift in the pulpit placed him among Dad's favorite guests.

Dad was a giant among preaching giants, but I never heard him boast of his own gift.

When I entered the ministry, possessing just three sermons from my senior homiletics class, Dad sent books, and tapes. He answered questions and offered suggestions. He started my collection of great British preachers. He sent duplicates from his library, pointed me to great authors, and boxed up a couple sets of commentaries to jump-start my reference library. He gave me room to find my own style and voice. He encouraged me to think, to listen, to study, to preach the truth and "make it sing."

We talked before dawn every Sunday morning. We talked of family, and work, and plans, and preaching, always preaching. He asked about my message, and told me about his. He always answered the phone with excitement, as though I was the best call of the week. Then again, it was Sunday, and Dad was always excited on Sunday. I think it gave him a lift, no matter what was going on around him, to know that his son was stepping into a pulpit as he stepped up to read his text. For me, it was a weekly affirmation of love and calling. There was not a Sunday morning conversation that Dad did not end with three words: "Preach well, son." I still hear those words before the dawn on Sunday mornings, and I wish that I could call him to read a few paragraphs for his input.

Parkinson's put an end to Dad's preaching. It robbed him of his ability to connect the dots – to stay on point. It slowed down his processor. It clouded his clarity and numbed his sense of timing. He battled confusion, and then suffered the weakening of his booming voice until all that remained was a whisper. I have often wondered what he would have given if, like Samson, he had been given the chance, just one more time, to preach a message that brought a bit of heaven down to earth? I know of all the things he meant when he said, "I miss my life," preaching was near the top of the list.

Something of him preaches in me when Sunday comes and I open to a text. It's a different style, and rhythm, and generation, but something of him is present every time. It might be the turn of a phrase, a bit of humor, a pause, a gesture, or story. It might be something that came in the study, a reminder of one of J. Stuart Holden's sermons, or George Duncan's brilliant structure. It might be our shared love of that moment when one knows, "I was made for this." In any case, I know that when I preach, I do not preach alone. I hear the echoes of my father.

It's Saturday, as I write these words. Earlier, I did one final edit on the message for tomorrow and looked for Dad in what I wrote. I found him in the way I opened, heard him in a pointed phrase, invoked his command and timing, and missed him desperately on the eve of another Sunday – the day he lived a little bit more than all the rest.

CHAPTER 12# The Study

D ad never pursued a post-graduate degree. His diploma from Central Bible Institute served him well. He studied beyond the classroom, almost every day of his life, building an outstanding library numbering more than three thousand preaching volumes–volumes he knew intimately. He loved study and labored over manuscripts. He read widely among Catholics, Presbyterians, Revivalists, Methodists, Pentecostals, Baptists, and Anglicans. He loved the minister's workshop. He was a master of dispensational eschatology, a student of divine providence, a collector of great preaching, and a teacher of homiletics.

Dad hand-printed rough notes in neat block letters, never rushing or scribbling. With notes in hand, he turned to the typewriter, and later the computer, to hammer out his own unique cross between outline and manuscript. Dad believed that words were powerful and precise instruments to be wielded with a surgeon's care. He was a master of phrasing, setting words in a deliberate order and cadence for maximum effect. He believed that the preacher must be a herald, an oracle, a spokesman for God. As such, the minister could not be excused to wander aimlessly, or swing wildly in the throws of emotion as he navigated a sacred text. His sermons never had to go searching for a plot or grasping for a thought. To Dad's way of thinking, the preacher was responsible to present a message born of study, spirit, intellect, sweat, and tears. The effective message was the end product of life, prayer, the Word, the times, the climate, and the study.

Preaching intensity is often misinterpreted as anger. Dad learned early on to use his natural gift of humor for balance and warmth, to modulate his voice and emotions. He collected stories, especially those invested with humor, and weaved them into the seams of a message, like pressure vents. He was a funny guy. He loved to laugh, and to make people laugh, but he never lost sight of the message for a story or a laugh. Some of his humor was planned, but much of it happened in real time as he connected with an audience. He laughed at himself, not at others, and accentuated positive themes, though he could lower the boom when the text did the same. His style was his own, although bits of C.M. Ward and Billy Graham leaked out in his speech, and E. Stanley Jones, J. Stuart Holden, James S. Stewart, and even Chuck Templeton might whisper from the shelves of his library.

Dad was energized in the study. I think he loved a message in its preparation as much as in its presentation. I never asked about an upcoming Sunday that he did not know what his message would be. I never knew him to dread the pulpit. For thirty years we talked about what we would preach. After retirement it was about what I would preach.. and then Parkinson's corrupted our connection and he lost the ability to focus – to follow – to connect the dots.

I felt the loss of that Sunday connection, as did he. For years, he had talked with his preacher/father, Clifford Crabtree, every Sunday. It just so happened that the week his father passed, I stepped into my first pulpit. Dad always felt that a torch was passed when he dialed my number that Sunday in May of '81.

As I finish my weekly preparation I often think how nice it would be to dial him up and test a few phrases, or share a new author, or pray for God's blessing on the brick and mortar behind a pulpit ministry. But our temporary disconnection leaves me only with the memories of what he said, how he said it, and how much he loved this preaching life.

From my father I learned to love the study, to seek out good resources, to use proper language, to illustrate with simplicity, to color with humor, to structure after the text, to preach for a decision. I learned it all as an apprentice in my father's workshop–the preacher's workshop. I think the lessons serve me well, and if not, fault cannot be found in my teacher. The love we shared in the sermon quest endures. The torch still burns brightly, and it remains for me to study hard, finish well, and before I go–pass it on. Last night my daughter sent a two-minute video of my four year-old Grandson, David, preaching to his twin brother and two year-old sister. I think the boy just might have what it takes!

Chapter 13

Failure

It was a Thursday in 1984. Cheri and I had just arrived in Des Moines for a weekend with Mom and Dad. Dad met me at the door and suggested we go to his office for a few minutes. It was odd. Something was off. We rode in silence and stepped through the back door into his book-lined study. I wasn't at all prepared when he said, "I've committed adultery. I'm through as a minister. You're going to have to step up and be the head of this family." He asked me to stay with him as he made a few last calls. I sat in stunned silence as he called key staffers and leaders. A funeral pall fell over that place. After completing one last call to our national overseer, he grabbed his keys and we went back to all that remained of home.

What do you do when it's your fault, when excuses ring hollow, when your nightmare escapes the dream realm and nothing you can do can make it go away? What can you do when you've taken yourself out, when your losses are compounding and there is no easy fix? What remains for the man or woman who has put everything that matters at risk – and lost? What do you do when you look in the mirror and see a fool, a hypocrite, a liar, a cheat? What do you do when your sin finds you out? You suffer, that's what you do. You pay an awful price. You bleed inside. You age a decade in a day. You want to die. You are alone with yourself – and you despise yourself. The verdict is guilty – no chance of appeal. Your pain is made worse by the knowledge that the pain you have inflicted is deeper still. What do you do when you've cratered your family and forfeited the ministry? You suffer, and in your suffering you repent, you apologize, you humble yourself, you let good people help you, you answer tough questions, you accept responsibility… and you get up off the mat. That's what I learned from my Father when he fell.

We suffered those dark days. We lived with Dad's embarrassment, Mom's betrayal, his humiliation, her shock and anger, their long and difficult reconciliation, a shared family journey back to life, health, and love. It was not easy or clean. God's grace is perfect but the way of the transgressor is hard and messy. It was dark, it was bleak, it was ugly, and at times it seemed that it was over. I wondered what our family would look like after the fallout. I wondered if the marriage could survive. I wondered how we would celebrate the holidays and what we would tell the grandchildren. I wondered at the devastation. Adultery is an untethered wrecking ball in a house of fine china.

Thirty years married, my parents started over from a dark, dark place. It took three years to stabilize and restore their broken relationship. Dad found success in sales and management, and then moved on to enjoy a season of ministry with Reach the Children. Although Dad engaged in limited preaching and teaching, a decade would pass before he found himself in the familiar weekly rhythm of pastoral life. Everything had been burned to the foundations.

Exiled from the only lives they had ever known, my father and mother had to feel their way in the dark and learn to live again... to love again. They grew stronger with each passing year, and at the age of sixty-two, against all odds, they returned to the pastoral life they so dearly loved. They picked up the pieces, began again, fulfilled their calling, and finished strong.

I was visiting Mom and Dad in Florida a couple of years before Dad died. He was feeble by then, wearied in the fight against Parkinson's disease. I had busied myself for most of the day with the small maintenance tasks he could no longer perform. I watched my mother as she cared for my father. I watched them together, how he looked at her, how she touched his shoulder. I saw the power of a sacred bond. I could almost hear a whisper from a distant altar, "in sickness and in health, to love and to cherish, 'til death." He lavished praise on her. She loved him, fought for him, fed him, kept him, and, at times, helped carry him when Parkinson's put him on the floor. He marveled at her strength as his was ebbing away.

I sat up late that night. The house grew quiet and I thought of the dark days – the stark days – those hard memories stored in a room I rarely visit anymore... and I thought of what I had witnessed as I puttered around playing handyman. The words escaped my lips to no one listening, "just look at how she cares for him... how my mother loves my father," and I understood the sacred vow in a deeper dimension–a sweeter frame–than I had ever known.

Failure is not fatal. Grace knows no limits. The roots of love grip deeper than imagined. We can begin again. Dad proved these things and more. He got up when he had fallen. He made it right – He made it back – He finished strong.

CHAPTER 14

Unpacking a Promise

Somewhere in the early aftermath of my father's affair, we talked of future ministry – a very dim prospect. I promised Dad that if he re-entered full-time ministry, I would be there for his first Sunday back in the pulpit. That promise was boxed up, like the bulk of his library, with no certainty that it would ever be unpacked. It lay dormant for ten years.

In 1995 Dad was called to the pastorate in Worcester. The timing was bad for me, with church and family obligations. I almost missed it. I almost stayed home to preach in my own pulpit, but as Dad and I chatted on a Friday he was setting up his office. He couldn't hide his excitement and I couldn't stand to be away. When I put down the phone, the promise that had only whispered in my conscience began to shout. Without telling Dad, I booked a last minute flight, bunked in a nearby hotel, and waited for the snowy dawn of a February Sunday morning in Worcester, Massachusetts.

I wasn't prepared for New England winter. I had to clear the snow off my rental with a rolled newspaper and my room card before making my way to the morning service. I arrived late and was greeted with a perfunctory handshake and practiced thrust of a church bulletin. The congregation was singing as I looked for Mom from the back of a dark sanctuary. Spotting her near the front, I slipped unnoticed into her row and put my arm around her shoulder. She startled and looked up, wondering just who this overly friendly New Englander might be. Her smile was worth it all. Dad's grin from the platform told me that he remembered – he was pleased. It was the first of many wonderful moments for our family at Worcester First Assembly of God.

Not many ministers make it back from moral failure. Families dissolve. Hopes are discouraged. Some argue that grace is sufficient and restoration is the goal. Others argue that the fallen should not aspire again to the pulpit, given the damage to testimony and increased exposure to litigation should trouble come again. Restoration programs are all over the map. Most don't have much to offer in the way of program or restoration. It's a chancy business for a church to take on a restored minister. It's a daunting challenge for a minister (the ministry is tough enough without baggage). Ministry places a strain on marriage in the best of cases. It calls for youthful energy to pull a church out of winter into spring. Dad and Mom were sixty-two and the church was in a difficult place. In the eyes of many, they were a long shot.

After a warm introduction, Dad stepped to the pulpit and settled his notes. I think I saw his lip quiver a bit, and then I heard that unmistakable voice... strong, deep, and sure. He read a text, paused for a moment, and launched his message. He was in a new place, yet completely at home–at home in the pulpit. I'm so glad I kept my promise. I cannot remember those moments, though years have passed, without smiling a smile that pulls at the depths of my soul.

CHAPTER 15

The Gold Star

Each year Cheri and I made a trip to Worcester for a holiday or get-a-way, always enjoying the change of pace and style New England offers a Southerner. We would drive through quaint villages, enjoy Mom's outstanding cooking, eat fresh fish at the Sole Proprietor, pray for snow, and revel in the warm embrace of the church that so graciously welcomed Mom and Dad.

When visiting, I fell into Dad's morning ritual with ease. Up at four-thirty – to the gym at five o'clock. After a workout, it was off to the Goldstar, a Worcester hole-in-the-wall lunch counter where Dad blew his workout by ordering corned beef hash. Then we might ride down the street to Starbucks for a Macchiato savored at a corner table before stopping at the church to check in with the crew at the office. The ritual was rarely interrupted or modified for a decade, except for every August, when the owner of the Goldstar would go home to Greece and leave the Worcester brain trust to fend for themselves for thirty days.

At the gym, Dad got on a bike, a treadmill, or an elliptical trainer, and ground out a steady rhythm. I would grind along from the next machine and remember the days I watched him jog around the cinder track at Greendale. He loved to work up a sweat. It was a near religious experience for him, like savoring lobster or the first sip of coffee on a cold morning. He loved to push a little further, to go another five minutes, to give it one last dig before heading to the shower and taking on the day. Dad knew and greeted all the regulars. He walked in every morning with a warm smile in the company of our friend, Ed Laughlin. I was always introduced with pride. I felt that same pride in Dad as I watched him work the room and jump-start his aging frame.

After a shower, we descended upon the Goldstar–a classic New England breakfast experience. The Goldstar was situated in a stand-alone one-story brick storefront encircled by snow-clogged sidewalks. The corner entry was cut at a forty-five degree angle and bells dinged on the door with the comings and goings of the morning rush. It was always warm and steamy except for the occasional frigid blast that would race across your ankles when the door was opened on a snowy day. The vinyl booths and linoleum floors dated back to the fifties. It was the kind of place Mom hated, a place where nobody ever heard of gluten-free, where the waitresses called everybody "dear" without the 'r. Dad was never so at ease as when he held the booth in the back at Goldstar with a steaming cup of coffee awaiting his beloved corned beef hash with his buddy, Ed. I loved the place.

Starbucks, after Goldstar, was like Macy's after Wal-Mart, but Dad always added that stop for me. He ordered his Grande Carmel Macchiato with a warm smile for the inked and pierced barista frothing milk and pulling shots. He was easy company.

Once at the office, Dad would check emails and letters, review the schedule with his assistant, Donna, show me a book or place a few calls before we returned to the house where my Mother and my wife expressed perpetual gratitude at their exclusion from our morning ritual.

If our paths should ever cross in Worcester – I know the odds are long – you'll find me in the morning, around six forty-five, in a back booth at Goldstar with a cup of steaming coffee and an order of corned-beef hash. Feel free to slide in, forget about cholesterol, and order up. Oh… and please don't order quiche.

CHAPTER 16

Christmas

Dad loved Christmas. He always put out a light show. He prided himself in finding just the right gift for Mom. He was animated, excited, warm and inviting. He was generous and fun loving. He was Christmas. He was always on the top of his game on Christmas morning, rising early to brew coffee and help Mom with the last minute details. He always read the story from Luke's gospel with his "God" voice. We prayed and gave thanks for family, whether present or abroad. His voice would catch with a bit of emotion. It was real.

Dad loved to carve the Christmas turkey and did nothing to dispel the myth that this skill was acquired by some rigorous apprenticeship. I grew up believing that turkey carving was a task performed best by men equipped with properly aged carving knives and a God-given intuition as to the proper way to parti-tion the yuletide bird. I cannot begin to describe the confusion of my first hacking attempts to match my father's artistry. Dad's Christmas platter looked like a

Hallmark card. My bird looked as though it had been caught in a fan.

As I write, it is two days before Christmas – our first without Dad. Mom is here, and my sister, Susan. My daughter, Lindsay, is back from the Philippines with a boyfriend in tow. Brandin and Lauren, my middle daughter and son-in-law, will be at our table. Phillip and Ashley, our firstborn and her husband, just arrived with David, Keegan, Brooklyn, and Selah, our magnificent grandchildren. We'll miss Mark and Beth and the rest of the Boykin's, but we'll be in touch by phone. We'll talk to our extended family across the nation. We'll feed off the energy of four grandchildren under the age of five, all primed and ready for an assault on the stash under the tree. But first, we'll sit down and enjoy the warmth of a Christmas hearth and I'll open Dad's preaching Bible to the second chapter of Luke's gospel. I'll read… and we'll cry… and remember. We'll open the gifts… and remember. We'll set a Hallmark table for a Christmas feast… and remember.

If heaven offered a furlough to those who have gone before, a single day to visit those left behind, I have no doubt that Dad would choose to join us on Christmas morning. I can well imagine him telling the stories he told us a hundred times or more. I can see him enjoying everything from the fire, to the coffee, to the kids, to the presents, to Lindsay's boyfriend, to whirling grandchildren, to Mom's new haircut. He would come in loud wearing a bright sweater to putter around the kitchen taste-testing everything. He would read the Christmas story and we would revel in the blessing he would offer in his prayer. I would gladly step aside and let him carve the turkey and sit at the head of our table. If only heaven offered a furlough. But heaven has no furloughs and I'm left to hope that something of Dad's anointing has fallen on me – that I'll somehow get it right – that my grandsons and granddaughters will see the joy of Christmas in me.

So, I'll be up early to brew the coffee and light the fire, to do the lifting and wrapping as needed, to plug in the lights and set out the family Bible, to putter around the kitchen and taste-test everything, to make Christmas a memory not soon forgotten, to fully embrace a legacy of laughter and love.

CHAPTER 17

The Ambulance Chaser

Dad had not been feeling well for about three days when Mom found him sitting quietly in the den. "You look a little grey," she said, "How do you feel?" Dad was never one given to complaint, so it jolted Mom when he said, "I feel like there's a Mack truck sitting on my chest." Mom dialed his doctor's office and handed him the phone to answer the nurse's questions. He looked up at my mother, covered the mouthpiece and said, "The ambulance is seven minutes away."

The parsonage was situated across from the Lincoln Street School on a short lane that opened into the church parking lot. The morning school traffic was non-stop. Watching from a front window, Dad saw the ambulance roll by, missing the house, and heading down the lane towards the church. Before Mom knew what was happening, he bolted, rushing down the front steps waving his arms. He was chasing his own ambulance.

After looping through the church parking lot, the ambulance driver spotted a silver-haired man in a tracksuit waving frantically. The driver and his partner pulled up to the parsonage and ran to open the rear doors. Dad reached in to help them with a gurney saying, "I think you're looking for me." Everything stopped for a moment, a moment that should have been captured on video.

The Emergency Medical Technicians asked him to stop helping, strapped him to the gurney, slammed the doors, and headed for the Medical Center with lights and siren. By the time Mom reached the hospital, Dad was already receiving the first of five stents. Dad was seventy-five.

He was released on the following Friday and terribly upset when his doctor forbade him to preach that Sunday. He stood at the den window and watched cars filling the parking lot at the end of the lane. He took his orders like a good soldier and suffered as only a preacher can suffer on a Sunday morning without a pulpit. On the next Sunday, he was back.

In short order, he was back in the gym, back to Goldstar, back to his corned beef hash, back in stride – albeit, a bit slower than before. I noticed something a bit off on my next visit, but put it down to the heart attack and to aging. Mom saw it too, and even his doctor wondered if he might be showing some early signs of Parkinson's disease. A battery of tests could not confirm a diagnosis and life quickly found its rhythm again.

Dad retired at seventy-six and I journeyed north with Cheri to help him pack up for the move south. Stepping into a half-packed house, I was alarmed to watch Dad struggle to focus and finish. Something was wrong; something beyond the emotional trauma of retirement. I took over, and with the help of a great team of friends, we closed up the truck and a final chapter in ministry. Dad climbed up into the cab beside me for our long journey south to Floridian sunshine. Cheri and Mom followed in the car.

I drove and we talked a bit. He slept a lot. We ate at Cracker Barrel restaurants and searched out the occasional Starbucks. We talked of fishing trips, bike trips, mission trips, mountain trips, beach trips... life was a trip. We talked of summers on Lake Lucerne, foggy Saint John mornings, Grand Manan Island lobster, Cape Breton Island camping, Des Moines First Assembly, Stockton, Delray Beach, Worcester, and Greensboro. We planned a few new adventures, talked about the places he wanted to see again, and wondered what retirement would look like when the truck was unpacked and the moving dust settled.

He was an old man who climbed down from the truck in Boca Raton on New Year's Eve. He shuffled a bit and tired quickly. His face took on a slightly confused expression. His eyes would lock and stare. An occasional tremor shook his right hand. He leaned a bit forward when he walked and his arms didn't swing in sync with his gait. He was a few days gone from the pulpit – a few miles away from family – a few months removed from a diagnosis that would shape his last fight and write his last chapter. I saw the signs, but hoped that a little rest would set him to rights. Those hopes were never fully realized. For our family, it was a New Year, a new place, a new phase in life, and a stark new reality. Dad was fading before our eyes.

CHAPTER 18

A Slow-Motion Robbery in Broad Daylight

When Dad was diagnosed with Parkinson's disease in 2009, it didn't come as a complete surprise. A doctor in Massachusetts had seen enough to run tests a few but couldn't reach a clear diagnosis. When that awful disease was finally unmasked, it rewrote Dad's retirement script and ushered us into a bleak and unmapped world. When he stepped onto the elevator, having received the diagnosis, he felt that his life was over. Parkinson's doesn't write a happy ending.

To this point, chronic disease had been a stranger to our home. Of multiple prescription drugs, clinical trials, medical supply companies, specialists, therapists, tremors, freezing, and falling, we knew nothing. Sickness, in our household, had been episodic and short-lived. Dad bounced back from his heart attack. We expected nothing less but you don't bounce back from Parkinson's. You manage Parkinson's – and Parkinson's manages you.

I saw Dad, on average, three or four times per year after his retirement. My sporadic visits had an accelerating effect similar to time-lapse photography. When I first started visiting Mom and Dad in retirement, Dad was always framed in the doorway, or standing in the driveway waiting for me. But as time went by, I would get further and further into the house before we met. Then we reached that point where he couldn't come to the door anymore, and I would find him in his chair, looking out over the back patio – looking small.

His face lost all expression. His shuffle became more pronounced. His balance failed. His feet would freeze in place. Confusion set in as his thought processes slowed. Trains of thought decoupled or derailed. His great voice abandoned him, retreating to a hoarse whisper. He began to fall and grew increasingly uncomfortable in crowds, or in fast-moving conversations. Loud sounds were magnified and light intensified until he was rarely without his dark glasses (I called him Mr. Onassis).

Parkinson's worked towards a complete isolation. The last two years were hard. His body threw off weight until nothing fit anymore. Muscles atrophied revealing a small boney frame. Every visit was a bit of a shock for me.

He never complained, only saying that he missed his life. He kept his sense of humor. He praised my mother for all that she did, marveling at her strength. He kept fighting until he had nothing more to give. He slowly faded away.

A million Americans suffer with Parkinson's disease. Some experience violent tremors, others suffer a decline in mental faculties, still others lose mobility, expression, and voice. Parkinson's is a disease of a hundred faces and a thousand symptom combinations. It's a slow-motion robbery in broad daylight. Some sufferers find measurable relief in drug treatments. If Dad's considerable drug regimens had any affect, we were unable to find the measure. From well before the day of Dad's diagnosis, Parkinson's was on the march and we struggled to match its cadence.

I don't consider Dad's death a victory for Parkinson's disease. He died fighting, and loving, and praying, and hoping. Parkinson's marched my father into a small, dark, place... but from that place, he made his great escape.

I'm retracing the steps we walked together down the Parkinson's road. I can't escape that dreadful disease. Five of my friends are presently fighting the same foe, and I can't walk with them or talk with them without a flood of memories drenching my soul. We talk often. We talk about Dad. We talk about faith, and courage, and strength. I pray I'll yet see a miraculous recovery–a stunning reversal–a complete restoration. If not, I'll wait with growing anticipation for the hour when Parkinson's stumbles into an eternal night, and we run on to awaken the dawn.

CHAPTER 19

Finally Home

It was a Saturday night, and Cheri and I were on our way home after dinner at a friend's house. It had been a wonderful evening. Our friends had extended the invitation sensing that we might need some fellowship, given my father's sharp decline. We had raised our children together, and now we were sharing the realities of caring for aging parents. We talked at length about my father, his recent trauma, and rapid deterioration. I had seen him four weeks previous and his weight loss and increased disorientation were heartbreaking. In the intervening weeks, he had slipped into unconsciousness one afternoon, necessitating a trip to the hospital. He had awakened, but never truly recovered. Hospice stepped in with remarkable tenderness and grace. It was a matter of weeks we were told.

As we drove, I was gripped by an impulse—strong and unshakable—that we should drive through the night to be at Dad's side. I called Mom and asked if we should come. Mom, ever the preacher's wife, suggested that we stay and take care of the church on Sunday and maybe come Monday. I hung up and we drove in silence for a few minutes before that same prompting returned with greater intensity. I had little doubt that this was God's grace to us. I called my associates to cover my Sunday responsibilities, called Mom to say, "we're coming," stopped long enough to load a few necessities, and drove through the night to arrive at Dad's doorstep mid-morning. For following that prompting, I was able to be with him for his last day.

After sitting at Dad's bedside for a while Sunday, I took a short bike ride to clear my head. On my return, I looked in on him and told him that I missed him on the ride (we share some great bicycle memories). His eyes opened, only for a moment, and then closed again, but there a flash of recognition. It is the only physical sign that offered any evidence that he knew I was even there. It's enough for me.

Monday morning something was different. You could sense it more than see it and I called for local family members to gather, though our caregivers thought it might be a bit premature. We surrounded his bed, and sang, and prayed, and cried. We told him again that he was dearly loved, and free to go. We told old stories and filled the house with laughter and hugs. We held his hands and watched his chest rise and fall in a room filled with love.

It was afternoon and his pulse was fading as family members rotated in and out. I was holding his hand. He took a couple of deep breaths, his eyes opened, and the hint of a smile, long held captive by

Parkinson's disease, escaped to touch the corners of his mouth for just a moment – and he was gone – and I knew in a new dimension, what Paul meant when he asked, "O death, where is thy sting? O grave, where is thy victory?" That moment was touched with eternal wonder. At the risk of being misunderstood, I must say that his moment of passing was one of the great moments of my life – as it was for him.

The inevitable sadness of separation was muted by the unsearchable richness of God's grace, presence, comfort, sovereignty, and joy. The certainties of faith in forever placed Dad at the top of my list of people I want to see when I take my final flight. He changed his address. I changed my frame of reference. Death's darkness could not find him... and it shall not find me.

When we are born, doctors, nurses, and parents anxiously await the child's first breath. When we die in Christ, I believe Heaven joyfully awaits our last. Among my mother's favorite lyrics are those of L. E. Singer in what became a song titled, *Finally Home*:

But just think of stepping on shore and finding it heaven;
of touching a hand and finding it God's;
of breathing new air and finding it celestial;
of waking up in glory and finding it home.

CHAPTER 20

The Ruddy Good Looks
of an Actor

Nobody knew or loved my father like my mother. She was a full partner in every aspect of his life. I saw them at their best. I saw them at their worst. I saw them build and burn: I also saw them sift through the ashes, pick up the pieces, and rise again. What I saw marked me for life. They wrote quite a story together, but you should hear it in Mom's own words:

It really wasn't love at first sight for David and me. I found him interesting. I was impressed by his love and respect for his parents and their long years in ministry. He was nice, kind, thoughtful, generous, and often the life of the party. Within about four months of dating, we knew that we were in love. My family loved him. We both felt called to ministry and started making plans together. I knew he was called to preach, and I thought that I could provide a music backdrop that he would love and support... and he always did.

We almost got to celebrate sixty years of marriage. During these years we raised three fine children, welcomed six amazing grandchildren and four great grandchildren. We enjoyed a lot of opportunities, travel, and victories. But we also walked some dark valleys. We suffered loss. But somehow we knew, somewhere, there would be a bright tomorrow… and there was.

David never blamed or complained. He always took pride in study, in writing, cleaning the garage, shoveling snow, cultivating his prized tomatoes, or planting thirty-three rose bushes for me. He did it right.

We both loved the pastorate and didn't want to retire, but we knew it was time.

We hoped to do some interim pastoral work. He didn't care how small the church or how far we might have to drive, he wanted to preach. When Parkinson's invaded our lives, that plan faded away. I watched the disease take its toll. One day he handed me the car keys and said, "You are my designated driver." Then, even the walks we enjoyed through our neighborhood became impossible. We were housebound.

He would watch preaching on TV and online. I would see tears well up in his eyes when great truth was powerfully communicated. Beth put together CD's of his favorite songs and we played them each night to help him go to sleep.

On March 24, 2014, three generations surrounded his bed with singing as he took his flight. His day nurse stood in the doorway weeping. She loved Mr. David. She hugged me and said, "I've never seen anything like this." God's presence filled the house and I understood, "Precious in the sight of the Lord is the death of his saints."

In 1980 the Des Moines Register featured a special weekend section on preachers and preaching. David was the first one mentioned. The religious editor had interviewed David, and in his closing paragraph he said, "David Crabtree has the ruddy good looks of an actor, the voice of an orator, and he preaches with fire and brains." I loved that! It was true!

My memories are dearer, my family closer, and my friendships are more meaningful now. Heaven is more real to me, and nearer than it has ever been. The name David means beloved. He was, he is, and forever will be. I love you David Crabtree.

David and Dawn Crabtree

CHAPTER 21

Dear Grandpa

My youngest daughter, Lindsay Crabtree, serves as an Assemblies of God Missionary in Baguio, Philippines. Dad was proud, as he was of all six of his grandchildren. Upon hearing of her grandfather's passing, and knowing that it would not be possible to attend his funeral, she penned the following letter. It was printed on Dad's funeral program.

Dear Grandpa,

Yesterday you "cross'd the bar" and finally saw your Pilot face to face. When Dad called me on Skype so I could say good-bye to you, there was so much I wanted to say. But I was crying too hard, so I only croaked out a few sentences. This letter is what I wanted to say. I know you can't read it, and even if you could, I wouldn't want to tear your attention away from the new life you're experiencing even for a second. This letter is for me to grieve and process through my language—writing.

This letter is a tribute to the gentlest, sweetest, funniest, most humble man of God I've ever known.

Even though I saw you via Skype just before you passed, I will never picture you as that old, emaciated man lying in the hospital bed. Every time I think of you, I see a man who is larger than life, bursting into the house when the girls and I were little, delighting in our shrieks of joy. I hear your deep, rich voice—not that breathy whisper that you had in your last days—telling stories with impeccable timing. And I can see the rest of the family sitting around, holding our sides from laughing so hard. After you reach the punch line, that laugh that was your trademark explodes out of you, like you just can't hold it back any longer. I see you leaping over those three rows of choir risers at Calvary. That's my grandpa.

I remember camping at Cherokee, Tennessee–walking out of the camper to see you sitting with your toothbrush hanging out of your mouth and toothpaste foam all over the place. The girls and I just collapsed in giggles. You went down to the creek with us. The water was ice-cold–I remember that. The girls and I were taking baby steps, gingerly sticking our toes in when you charged by and flung yourself right down into the icy water. You didn't even flinch, and we thought you were super-human. We have great pictures from that trip. The girls and I are smiling so hard it looks like our faces will split. And you are sitting right in the middle of us, a huge grin on your face, flashing a thumbs-up at the camera. I look at that picture and hear your laughter. What an amazing grandpa.

So many memories. All of your stories about your many years as a Pastor. Your dry sense of humor. Those cowboy boots you'd wear—you swore you couldn't get them off yourself, so the girls and I would yank them off, laughing the whole time. When you'd sleep in the waterbed and call us girls in to pull you out. That one time we girls and Aunt Susan decided to burst into your room in the middle of the night and jump on your bed—I won't tell the rest of the story, but it was hilarious. The time you forgot to sing The Lord's Prayer at the end of Christmas Eve service. We all thought Nana would have your head for that one! Your habit of reading signs out loud in your magnificent voice. This is just the tip of the iceberg.

My most recent memories include my college days. I would drive down to Boca from Lakeland to spend the weekend with you and Nana. Every morning while I was there, you would make me coffee and a bagel with cream cheese and jam. You just loved doing something for me. The last time I talked to you on the phone, your voice was barely a whisper. You said, "Love you, Linds... we're proud of you." I love you, too, Grandpa.

Parkinson's took a lot away from you... your facial expression, your voice, your sense of adventure, your strength, your abilities... your life. Although you became so much smaller physically, you were never diminished in my eyes. Parkinson's couldn't take away your hero status. You taught me so much.

From you, I learned about having a sense of humor and being able to laugh at myself. I learned about faithfulness in ministry. I learned that life is one grand adventure. I learned about the faithfulness and restoration of God. I learned about falling down and getting back up. I learned about hard work and determination. I learned about loving your family. How you loved your family! You raised two wonderful, godly daughters and an incredible, godly son who is the best Dad in the world—probably because he had the best Dad in the world. When I think of integrity and godliness and a gentle heart, I think of my grandpa. Parkinson's took a lot from you, but yesterday, God took you away from Parkinson's. "Death shall have no dominion." It is all victory!

For those of us left behind, life will go on. For you, life has just begun. I am so happy for you, and I would not call you back to this earth for a second—not even for one last hug and big kiss on the cheek. You always were larger than life, and that is truer now than ever. When I get to heaven, I want to see Jesus and hear, "Well done, good and faithful servant." But the second thing I want to hear is your booming laugh.

John Donne wrote, "One short sleep past, we wake eternally, And death shall be no more; Death, thou shalt die." I am waiting for that day when I will wake up in eternity and see you again.

I love you. I'll see you soon.
Your ever-adoring granddaughter,
Linds

CHAPTER 22

On Pamlico Sound

Crossing the Pamlico Sound for a few days of solitude on Ocracoke Island, I'm purposely going to a place Dad and I shared, and loved. The ocean never had a better friend than Dad. He loved the wind, the waves, the salt air, beaches, rocky outcroppings, dunes, and driftwood. We used to drop the tire pressure on my Subaru Outback and drive down the beach at low tide, once coming upon the partial skeleton of a sailing ship uncovered by a storm. We visited the lighthouses on Hatteras, Corolla, and Oregon Inlet. We ate conch fritters at Howard's Pub and marveled that the fish was always cooked to utter perfection. We watched schools of dolphins breaching the surface as though guarding the shallows. We sat in rockers on a second story deck and talked about nothing and everything until the light was gone and the sound of the surf promised the kind of rest you only know when you're disconnected from land and labor. Dad believed that the ocean could heal you… and tonight I'm hoping he was right.

The ocean didn't have to do a thing for Dad... he just loved to be near it, to feel the breeze, to gaze upon its nautical glories, to run the surf. He never lost his wonder of the ocean's immensity, its mystery, or restless motion. If he were riding the ferry with me tonight, he would be stretched out and smiling, watching the rise and fall of the horizon. He would remind me of another late night crossing when a ferryman, by chance, was reading one of my articles from an issue of the Pentecostal Evangel on his evening break... or coming back across with Ed after raising big bucks on the bicycle for a Christian School... or telling old stories to my riding partners to stave off nausea when the ship's roll took on a twisty motion... or maybe we would talk of that crossing we shared on a dark New Years Eve on the Bay of Fundy when he held me close as the MV Grand Manan dipped her railings in the waves and the captain later admitted his fear for the ship.

The last time we came here was the last time he was up to traveling alone. When I picked him up at the airport he couldn't hide his confusion. Parkinson's was steadily robbing him of his smile, his words, his connectedness, and his motion. We traveled deep into the Smokies for a chicken potpie at the Apple Barn– just because he loved the place–then crossed the state to traverse the outer banks from Ocracoke to Corolla. We couldn't walk the beach together anymore... but we could watch the waves. We couldn't go far or fast, as his strength would fade and his interest would waver, but we revisited the places we so loved. When I looked across at the aged man in the passenger seat,

I saw a face somewhat frozen and lifeless, empty-eyed and haggard. But there were moments... a picture against the backdrop of a fishing trawler... a handsome pose at the rail of the ferry... a grin as we slowly hiked back to the car on Mount Mitchell... a deep groan of satisfaction after biting into that first conch fritter at Howard's Pub... great moments and memories.

I'm thinking of him tonight... and wishing he were here with me on Pamlico Sound. In an hour we'll dock, and I'll check in to one of our favorite places for a few days of writing and planning. I'll drop my stuff and head for Howard's, where I'll order conch fritters, even though they're not good for me. I'll take a few pictures, so I can tell a few stories to my grandsons, and plan a trip I'll take with them sometime soon... a trip with Grandpa... to the great wide ocean where healing is easy—where hopes are rekindled, where adventure awaits, where I once shared life with my father, my friend.

CHAPTER 23

A Copse of Pine

I awakened to the kind of rain one only hears at the ocean–it roars–it slaps–it rages. I could hardly see across the tiny harbor for sheets of rain, grey ghosts on troubled waters. I came here to think, to pray, to write, to process my loss, to remember, to prepare for resurrection Sunday just five days away. And so, I made coffee and promised myself I would knuckle down and get things done.

I began in Daniel, tracing resurrection texts, to John's fifth chapter, Paul's letter to the Corinthians, then on to Revelation, where resurrection is a pretext for all yet to come. This is what Dad and I used to do each winter... steal away to some out-of-season inn with books and bikes and coffee and time... time for us.

"Let me see what you've written Dad," I said.

"Here's my hook, what do you think?" he would say.

"What if..." and we were off on the chase.

I looked up from Revelation. The rain had stopped and the wind was quick-drying the roads. Radar showed a brief gap in bands of rain–dark green on the radar with lumps of red and yellow. I decided to take a chance–to steal a bike ride on a rainy day.

Ocracoke Island is thirteen miles long and barely a mile at its widest point; a stubborn spit of sand between the Atlantic and the shore. To ride from the village to the ferry and back was a blessing and a curse. The wind, with gusts to thirty, was quartering at my back on the way out, and in my face on the way in. Four miles from the village the road intersects a copse of pine trees, strangely thick and tall on this island of scrub, grass, and dune. The pines cover the road like a canopy for a half-mile or so, and it was under the pines a forgotten moment was waiting.

Ten years ago, Dad and I got up early on Hatteras, took the ferry to Ocracoke, and unloaded our bikes at the landing to ride into the village for lunch. We pushed through the wind until we reached that same copse of pine where gathering clouds conspired to unload diluvial torrents. We were cold before the rain began and all thoughts of riding on to lunch were suddenly vanquished. It was decided that Dad would take shelter in the pines and I would ride hard to retrieve the car at the ferry landing.

My feet and hands were numb. I was soaked to the skin when I sloshed into the car park. Lashing the bike to the rack and cranking the heater to broil, I raced back to the pines. I was worried about my seventy-year-old father, soaked and shivering in a rain that blew sideways. The wipers were whipping in a vain attempt to clear the flood. I strained to see if I could pick him out of the grey. As I drew near, the wind tore a hole in the downpour and there he was, soaked to the bone, dragging his bike out to the roadway. His nose was bright red and dripping rain. His face was locked in a grimace or was a sly grin? We sat there for a moment, on the side of the road, roasting in a Subaru, under a pine tree canopy–and then, laughter... "Man, Dave," he said, "that was something else. We must be crazy."

I remembered that moment today as I pedaled through the same piney canopy... and the skies opened up and soaked me to the bone just four miles down with twenty-three to go. But it wasn't so bad, and I pedaled on in the wet warmth of April. I looked to the grey heavens, laughed like Dad, and cried a bit among the sodden dunes between the pines and the car park, so grateful we were never too busy to take time... for us.

CHAPTER 24

North

Dad slipped away gradually. Parkinson's slowed him down, dulled his senses, and then systematically robbed him of mobility, communication, desire, appetite, memory, and breath. For the last couple of years we haven't really been able to have a conversation, and over the last months he could only whisper... sometimes. He was still very much here, but I couldn't talk to him on Sunday mornings, or see what he thought of a grand adventure, or gain feedback on something I was working on. Maybe it was merciful in its way... our extended goodbye... maybe we grieved while he was yet with us... maybe we had a luxury many do not–time. Though I hate the disease, I have no angry complaint. Yet, I find myself trying to fully grasp the emotions, and their erratic interruptions, as a month draws near since Dad died.

My world is different. I'm only beginning to see what a powerful presence he was in my life. Dad wasn't paying my bills, or stoking my creative fires, or providing needed wisdom, or emotional support.

Dad was fighting Parkinson's, and, by his own words, "missing his life." I didn't need Dad for what he could give, or do, or say... he had given, and done, and said so much that my storehouse remains full... no, he was a central point of reference in my world. I wanted, everyday, to share my life with Dad, even if Mom had to relay the messages or show him the pictures when he could track with her. I knew that he was there... that I had roots... that I was loved... that someone wanted to hear from me. I touch a dozen touchstones every day that he helped fix in my soul. And now, he is gone. It is as if I gave someone my compass and they handed it back with South, West, and East in tact... but North is missing.

When it was time to sell our church property and relocate a few years ago, we discovered that our deed didn't close creating a barrier to the sale of the property. The old surveys referenced a rock, a tree, an existing iron pipe... but we couldn't identify the rock, or the tree, and the existing iron pipe didn't exist anymore. Two surveyors gave it their best shot without resolution. It escapes me as to how we got the deal through, but some kind of closure was negotiated. That's where I'm living–a central point of reference is missing and the resulting disorientation will only pass when God's infinite grace and mercy bring some measure of closure. I'm not struggling with my loss... it's more like a new dance. I'm not fighting rogue emotions... it's more like coffee with friends and an empty chair. I'm not wishing him here... just missing him here.

CHAPTER 25

30 Days

Has it been thirty days since you finished your race? It seems like forever... it seems like a day. I wish heaven had a general mail call–a little box office tucked behind the throne of grace where, having offered my praise and prayers, I might drop a note to you. I would tell you that Mom is strong–but you knew that. I would tell you that the girls are doing well, that we're stronger together for your passing– but you would have expected that. I would tell you how much you were loved–but you knew that. I would tell you how one memory has uncovered the next, and the next, until I have been laughing one moment and misting over the simplest things. I would tell you about Easter Sunday, and what a great day we had, and how strange it seemed when I could not place the call I have made for thirty-two years..."Happy Easter, Dad. He is risen!"

We're building a new normal–but you knew we would. You never oversold yourself as though the whole family would fall apart without you. You kept a humble heart and I think you knew your work was just about finished long before we were comfortable to think or say it. Our new normal holds deeper affection, greater respect, higher goals, open arms, and a path to follow. Our new normal is missing a central point of reference, but you were so consistent, we're finding our way–even in the dark. Our new normal is four, not five… but untroubled by Parkinson's… free from worries about you falling, or failing, or wasting away. Our new normal is going to be okay–but you knew that.

I wish you could write me just a few lines about His presence. I'd love to hear your booming voice say, "Dave, what a place!" I'm sure we've got it half wrong with harps and halos and streets paved with gold. But just knowing you're home there is more than enough. Just knowing you'll be there to welcome us makes heaven much sweeter and closer by far. So, I can't post my letter except to those living on this side of the veil, but in its writing I've found my heart a bit warmer, my hopes a bit higher, my peace a bit deeper, and my memories sufficient to fill the void.

Chapter 26

Sisters

I shared my father with two sisters. Neither carried the slightest hint of the tomboy, so I had Dad to myself for most of the guy stuff. Susan and Beth knew Dad in a different dimension. To me, he was Dad. To them, he was Daddy. Sons and daughters connect at different points to a father's heart. I think I understand my sisters better now, having raised three daughters of my own.

Susan was born in life-threatening crisis – a miracle baby. That she survived is a story in itself... that she has thrived is a testimony of God's grace and power. Those dark hours created a unique bond between Susan and Dad. I never resented it. I don't think I ever tried to put it into words. It was simply there.

I felt its slightest breath when my middle daughter, Lauren, took a fall and slashed her lip at two years old. We rushed to our doctor's office for stitches. They placed her little body on an examining table and brought in a couple of nurses to hold her still. That picture, etched in my mind, still breaks my heart. They placed a little hood over her head to isolate the wound. Suddenly, she couldn't see, and I broke protocol, gently moving a nurse to one side. I took Lauren's hand in mine and raised the hood until her eyes could see mine. We never looked away – not for a moment. She didn't see the doctor putting in the stitches. I didn't see anything but those big tearless eyes.

That was when I captured a hint of what my father and sister shared... it was a fellowship of suffering – a fellowship in suffering.

When Dad passed, Susan wrote:

> He was larger than life and his optimism was contagious. I can still see him throwing back his head in unbridled laughter. I can still hear his booming voice proclaiming the uncompromising Word of God with passion, humor and authority. Dad never knew I had cancer. It would have been too much for him in his fragile condition. And yet, it seemed when our eyes met, there was understanding we both knew suffering and wanted to do it with dignity. My heart is broken he is gone, but comforted in knowing he is with the One he has served, worshipped and adored. I will love you forever, Daddy. You will always be my hero.

Susan and I were separated by fifteen months. Beth followed me five years later. She was, in every way, the baby. She knew this by some intuitive gift, and milked it from early childhood. We antagonized each other – fighting to a draw. By the time a third child comes, the parents relax a bit. I have always thought my folks let Beth get away with murder, although I have never been able to locate a body. She was every bit of Daddy's little girl.

When I think of Dad and Beth, I hear laughter. She was joy to him. Her precocious talents brought him great pride. Her fighting spirit was a mirror reflection of Mom. He would quietly back away when they banged heads–a wise man. Dad did not spoil Beth... well, not too much. He enjoyed her.

I was at college when Beth hit her teen years. I dropped in for the summers to eat, sleep, and work. I watched my little sister grow up in spurts. As I pulled out of the driveway for my last semester at college, my baby sister waved from the side door. I never saw her again – that baby sister – that kid. I think she grew up the moment I drove away, becoming a strong woman, a brilliant musician, a wonderful caregiver, a trusted friend.

Beth was the onsite sibling for Dad's retirement years. She was magnificent in filling that difficult and demanding role. When Dad passed, Beth wrote:

It is no struggle to define my father, his personality, his character or his attributes. I never once wondered if Dad had the respect of his peers or his community–if he would do the right thing. The man he presented was the father I knew.

Dad was quick, decisive and always a sure thing. He was meticulous about all things, from his handwriting to his freshly pressed shirt collar. These were the little things that always gave me a sense of pride.

Dad was the man of common sense, in the mundane and in the complex. He could assess the problem, deal with it swiftly, and sleep like a baby. He never let us sulk. It was "brush yourself off and try again." Before the days of mandatory seatbelts, I recall my head hitting the console in the church van as we stopped a little suddenly. Dad simply picked me up, sat me back in my seat and said, "You're ok"... and I was.

I recall his '74 Thunderbird rolling into the church parking lot. I was chatting with a young man way past curfew. It was his low radio voice I heard: "Beth Anne, get in the car." That's all he needed to say.

Even with his meticulous nature, Dad could always lay things aside for a good laugh. His spontaneity could lighten the mood in the boardroom or the living room. He lived and loved in the moment.

Dad's decline brought us closer, my sisters and me, not that we have ever known estrangement. We have talked more, remembered more, savored shared moments more, tried to get together more, and enjoyed each other more. Dad gave us everything, and we all found our own ways to give back – wishing somehow we could have given so much more. It's a testimony to our father that in his passing we are not diminished, but stronger still and sharing more than we ever knew he had given to us.

CHAPTER 27

Legacy

My pastoral calling takes me far beyond personal precincts. I walk the pleasant paths and broken roads of a thousand legacies. I see the image of the father both revealed in virtue and twisted in vice. I counsel those who weep tears of joy and suffer blinding rage. I've heard both the grateful and the angry raise their voices in adoration or accusation describing their legacy with a single sentence, "I learned it from my father." I more often hear the counts of indictment rather than counts of blessing. A young man wears the legacy of abandonment. A mid-lifer struggles with scars left by abuse. A woman carries a graven image of selfishness, or indulgence, beneath a polished and fragile veneer. A young father describes his life in terms of his father's addictions or adulteries. The deepest lines are etched in the soul by a father's hand.

The first anniversary of my father's passing fast approaches and I am only beginning to take account of his legacy. The assets that follow are only a cursory inventory, but I think I've described the main categories in my father's bequest.

Faith: When, in younger years, I could have so easily walked away from God, the integrity of my father's faith held me fast. My creep towards agnosticism was always challenged by the reality he lived each day. He preached to me – a thousand times or more – but his life spoke louder than his sermons and I have eternity to show for it.

Family: I grew up in a pastor's home – a preacher's kid – a church rat. Stories of rebellion born of the parsonage were well known to me from my pre-teen years. Preacher's kids were supposed to be marred in some way by the experience of living in the ministry fishbowl. They were known for being rebellious, as Thomas was known for doubting. It was expected that there would be some blowback from living so close to the dark side of church folk. But in planning my own rebellion I found myself lacking the proper tools. I loved being a preacher's son. I loved our churched life. I loved the massive extension of family – the friendships born of the fellowship – the pride in my parent's leadership – the steady heartbeat of a healthy church. I never felt that I had missed a thing; that I suffered neglect; that I was less fortunate; that I was second to the ministry in the heart of my father. My rebellion fizzled for the lack of an antagonist. With Dad, family came first. It was a guarded priority. I have followed in echelon and my children have taken the same positive view of ministry. For this, I am forever in my father's debt.

Friendship: Dad loved people and enjoyed rich friendships. He didn't keep the congregation at arms length. Occasional wounds came as an occupational hazard, but Dad was willing to be wounded rather than live without friendship. He found friends in the ministry... friends in a rag-tag breakfast club... friends in the gym... friends of high and low estate. Dad knew that isolation was dangerous, stifling, and lonely. He knew that his batteries were charged by engagement with people. He was a good friend... especially to me. What I know of friendship, I first saw modeled by my father.

Exercise: Dad was a runner long before Frank Shorter, Bill Rogers, and Jim Fixx led the running revolution of the '70s. He loved the work, the sweat, the rhythm, the challenge of running a little further—a little harder—a little better. He often said that he didn't like running, but he loved having run. I knew what he meant, but I also spent enough miles at his side to know that he loved just being out there. For Dad, running was therapeutic. For me, his running was inspiring. I ran through high school and college. I ran to stay in shape and keep my weight under control. I ran for the joy of having run. I ran and raced everything from 5K's to the marathon, always thinking of Dad – always the little boy chasing my father around a black cinder track in Greendale – always smiling at the thought of his big burst at the finish – his laughter when he beat me there – his pride in me when I bested him that very first time. Running took a toll on my knees, so I took up the bike. Dad joined me there, and we rode, and worked, and sweat, and shared the miles until he just couldn't go any further. I still run a bit and ride a lot, and always will until I can't go any further. For this love, I owe my father.

Discipline: Dad followed through. He wasn't a perpetual starter. He finished. He was orderly, neat, organized, and meticulous. His study habits were deeply ingrained. His morning routines were inviolate. He knew that if he could get himself out the door and into motion, he would be a happier man for it. Dad wasn't sloppy about anything. He enjoyed long tenures in ministry, not jumping at any opportunity. He was deliberate and steady. Dad wasn't a sprinter – he was in it for the long run. He taught me that integrity is the key to longevity – that sometimes you have to outlast your problems – that hard work is worth it – that life's greatest joys are built on simple habits. This year I will celebrate my thirtieth year at the helm of Calvary Church. I learned to stick to it by following the disciplines of my father.

Enjoyment: Dad knew how to enjoy life whether it be the morning's first cup of coffee, or a brilliant sunset, or the artful turn of a phrase, or an old story, or a shared adventure, or sweat, or travel, or challenge. Dad was great at talking you off the ledges, or helping you gain perspective, or shaking you back to reality when emotions ran a bit wild. He avoided fanaticism, pessimism, and mysticism. He wasn't much for the weird or wild in spiritual matters. He stayed away from the spooks and the kooks. He didn't think that the enjoyment of God came at the cost of common sense. He saw life as a gift to be enjoyed rather than a mystery to be unraveled. He loved to point out that

Solomon, in all of his wisdom, found "three things too wonderful, four that he did not understand" (Proverbs 30:18). Dad didn't have to figure it all out, or dissect every mystery, or tie up all loose ends, or unravel the formulas. Dad always left room for wonder, knowing that without wonder there is no worship, and without worship life is meaningless. My father taught me to enjoy life – and people – and beauty – and God.

Preaching: I became what I never intended to be, a pastor. Some people might have expected my life to turn out this way. Two great-grandfathers were pastors. Two grandfathers were pastors. Three uncles are pastors or missionaries. Both of my sisters are engaged in full-time ministry. Two brothers-in-law, and four cousins are in the ministry. You could say that preaching was the family business and that my life-course was predictable. In my own analysis, there are two factors that led me into the ministry. First, I experienced the call of God at the age of seventeen and began running toward what I had been running from. Second, I grew up in the home of a great preacher/pastor and couldn't imagine giving my life to a greater cause. God called me. Dad showed me. In truth… two Fathers set the course of my life, and I am a forever grateful son of both.

Hope: In all my life I only knew my father to be down on two occasions, and he didn't stay down for long. Dad always looked up, reached up, and got up. He saw no redeeming purpose in whining, complaining, or groveling in self-pity. It was always going to get better. There was always a brighter day coming. It was always too soon to quit. There was always a reason for hope. He never allowed bitterness to take root in his soul. He didn't blame others. He saw life against the backdrop of eternity and decided that he just could not lose. Parkinson's is a terrible diagnosis for an eternal optimist. The progressive nature of the disease has a draining effect on hope. Mom always let me know if Dad seemed down, but when I called, he wouldn't play the martyr. No doubt that he had dark days, deep frustrations, and disappointments. But he was never disillusioned with his faith – even with the growing disintegration of his body. I learned to look up by following the eyes of my father.

Death: If Christ does not come soon, I will die. There is something about seeing your father die that erases all that remains of youthful illusions of immortality. But my father's death gave me far more than this. Dad's passing strengthened my faith, shattered my fears, and made heaven so near that I could never doubt its reality. Dad died at peace, surrounded by love, having lived a life that mattered. Dad died having said all the right things and settled all accounts. He died after blessing his family and changing his world. He died as he lived – on time. When that hour comes for me it won't be the stranger and I won't leave regrets. This parting gift from my father I cherish as the rest.

The man he was lives on in who I am–my father's son–the keeper of the flame–a living legacy.

CHAPTER 28

A Final Word

(Spoken at the Life Celebration for David C. Crabtree, March 30, 2014, Church of All Nations, Boca Raton, Florida)

I would be remiss were I not to express our deep appreciation and gratitude for the kindnesses shown to our family; for the memories you have stirred in our hearts; for sounding a final amen to a thousand things we knew and loved about Dad; for coming here today to offer the ultimate gift of presence.

I have collected a few minor honors in my life, represented by plastic trophies, wooden plaques, and yellowing certificates. All combined and multiplied by a million, they pale in comparison to the honor afforded me in this hour in offering a final word concerning the life of my father.

There is hardly a Bible text that I cannot hear my father's strong voice proclaim. I hear him when I read, "In the beginning." I hear him unveil Christ in Isaiah.

I hear him thunder in Revelation. I feel his timing and phrasing – the way he milked every word for its essence and quintessence–ever the orator. I can hear him read the text chosen for this occasion:

> *"Therefore, since we are surrounded by so great a cloud of witnesses, let us also lay aside every weight... and sin that clings so closely... and let us run with endurance the race that is set before us... looking to Jesus, the founder and perfecter of our faith... who for the joy that was set before Him endured the cross, despising the shame... and is seated... at the right hand of the throne of God."*
> Hebrews 12:1-2

Dad has joined that great company of the redeemed whose lives bear witness to the very possibility of the Christian life. The race *can* be won. The prize can be attained. I'm quite sure that those in that great cloud of witnesses do not watch us run. If there are grandstands in heaven, they must certainly encompass a celestial throne, not a sin-cursed world. The cloud of witnesses serves as examples, blueprints, and patterns for us to follow that we might finish well. My father has joined that august company.

It is impossible to sum up Dad's life with a single text, or context. He was a child of God, a first-born son, a husband and father, grandfather and great-grandfather. He was a mentor, a master, a student, a preacher, a teacher, a pastor, a confidant and friend. He was a writer, communicator, broadcaster, musician, athlete, gardener, outdoorsman, and cook. He was my best friend, my constant counselor, my greatest encourager, my running partner, my hero… my Dad.

He lived by words–a voice, calling men and women to a new life in Christ. He was eloquent and powerful, skilled and deliberate. His words are first remembered by most, and his manner of speaking suggests three lessons.

Say it well

For Dad, God's Word required proclamation. He had little patience with preaching that fell short of a sure declaration of essential truth. He wasn't one for quiet talks, or congregational conversations. I could never imagine my father closing a message by saying, "Next week we'll continue this dialog." He never got up to *share* a few thoughts. It was his conviction that if you dared to stand in the pulpit you had better have something to say, and since you were speaking for God, you had better say it well.

By the close of the message, he had sounded a trumpet call, or breached a fortress heart, or opened a way, or set something on fire. Under the anointing, he had spoken as the oracle of God and delivered an ultimatum. He didn't whisper in a dark room; he turned on the lights! He didn't have to preach; he got to preach! He didn't dread the study; he loved the quest! He labored to structure the message – carefully choosing language. He used stories and illustrations to open a window in someone's prison.

It all mattered to Dad... every phrase, every pause, every point, the introduction, and the invitation. He believed that if God's Word was proclaimed, God's power would infuse its declaration, God's presence would fill the house, and the triumph of the cross would pierce the darkest night of the soul. And so, because of His high regard for scripture, he demanded of himself, of his students, of all who sought his guidance... say it well!

Say it again

Dad loved great stories, and great stories demanded repetition. He loved to laugh, and when a story generated laughter, you can be sure that he would tell it over and over. He laughed every time—and it was genuine.

I invited Dad to join me on a two hundred mile bike trip nine years ago. Though he was then in his early 70's, he trained hard, turning his trip into a fundraiser for the Christian School in Worcester. My training partners were total strangers to Dad, for a couple of hours, and then he started telling stories—stories I had heard a hundred times before—and I elbowed my way in to find a place at the table. He had the guys laughing, and we laughed for three days and two hundred miles.

I watched my mother, who had heard the stories a hundred times more than me, and she would laugh every time. My girls always wanted Grandpa to tell the stories.

Two nights ago, as we gathered after his passing, we told the stories–the stories that make you smile–the stories that cause you to remember the love, the life, the lunacy, the legacy.

Dad believed that a good story could be told a thousand times or more. He believed that the ultimate story, the gospel, never got old.

He loved to preach the cross, though he had preached it a thousand times before. How he loved to preach redemption. How he loved to tell of the prodigal in the pigpen, or the woman at the well, or the beggar on the Jericho road. How he loved to craft a message for that moment of response–an altar call – where lives were changed.

I am one of an unknown number of younger men and women whose lives he touched; who stood at a sacred desk today to tell the story all over again. Somebody preached the prodigal. Somebody preached the blood. Somebody preached prophesy. Somebody preached providence. Somebody preached Paul in the jailhouse, or John on Patmos, or Jesus, our soon coming King! It thrills me today to think of those who stand in pulpits and classrooms because of a faithful pastor and mentor. We have stood as one to tell the old, old story again, and he would have loved that.

Say it now

Dad didn't bottle up praise or withhold affirmation. He never left people in the dark as to how he felt about them. He said it, and I'm the richer for it. As the disease progressed, and his need for help became more pronounced, he never failed to offer his care-givers a heartfelt "thank-you." He praised my mother to all who came near. "She takes such good care of me," he said.

Until conversation became impossible, we never signed off that he didn't say he loved me. Over the last 18 months, he said, and we said, the things we needed to say. When it was obvious that he would soon leave this earthly dwelling, I was talking with my sister on the phone as we made arrangements. I asked if she wanted me to hold the phone up to his ear, although we were not certain that he could hear us. Her response struck a common chord. "No, Dave, we've said it all."

We were left at Dad's bedside with a completed script. All the points were fully developed. The final sermon, that was his life, was finished. We could only say, "Dad, it's done, it's a masterpiece, and you can let go now."

I'll soon be leaving for a cross continental bicycle adventure across Africa. Because that ride is fast approaching, I brought a bike for training, and on the bike I've thought mostly of Dad.

Sunday, I rode and the wind was horrible. It shifted constantly and seemed to fight me all the way out and back. Arriving at the garage, his garage, I saw his bike leaning against a rack and I could see him there saying, "Man, Dave, what a wind... *that was great!*"

On Tuesday, somewhere near Boynton Beach, the sky turned black and the bottom fell out, and I found myself 18 miles from home and drenched. As I pedaled through that soup I felt him at my side saying, "Man Dave, what a storm... *this is great!*"

On Wednesday, I rode in the heat of the day, and suffered for it. I could picture him, outside the garage, pouring water over his head saying, "Man, Dave, what a scorcher... *that was great!*"

Last Monday, at 1:34, Dad took flight... and I wished that I could have had a day pass to heaven– to follow along–to see him standing at the gates of splendor as a Voice thunders: "Well done, good and faithful servant." I can see my dad take one last measure of his life, look over his shoulder at me and say, "Man, Dave, what a life... *that was great!*"

If life got tough, he looked up. If it needed saying, he spoke up. If you needed a friend, he stood up. When he fell down, he got up. When put to the test, he held up. When life was a mess, he picked up. When there was challenge, he stepped up. When charged with a cause, he signed up. When entering a room, he lit up. In good times and bad, he looked up. And when God called him home, he rose up.

The following poem is a Christianized version of Ella Wheeler Wilcox's *Resolve*. It marked him deeply. He committed it to memory... as have I.

Stand out in the sunlight of sorrow forgetting, whatever the past held of sorrow and wrong, we waste half our strength in a useless regretting, we sit by old tombs in the dark far too long.

Did you miss in your aim – well, the mark is still shining, did you fail in the race, then take breath for the next. Did the clouds drive you back, but see yonder their lining. Were you tempted and fell, let it serve as a text.

As each day hurries by, let it join the procession, of skeleton shapes that march down to the past, while you take your place in the line of progression, with your eyes on the cross and your face to the blast.

CHAPTER 29

At Dad's Grave

Seven months ago I walked a Floridian cemetery with my mother, to select a piece of ground in which to inter my father's spent body, and insure Mom's future place at his side. You don't prepare yourself for such moments – you don't know how to feel, or if you even feel at all – it's just grass, earth, wind, sun, sky... and grief. There wasn't much discussion, and I'm afraid I offered little more than mindless agreement as the plot was chosen and the sales representative, or family counselor, or client services specialist, or whatever he was rattled on in a vain attempt to be more than a stranger. I walked, a bit disconnected, fulfilling my role as a son to his father and mother – numb.

Then came the funeral, so great a celebration; so full of joy; such a sense of God, grace, and hope. At the funeral we said it, we sang it, with tears and triumph: "we will meet again, Dad." My memory of the funeral is so very warm – and that graveyard, so very cold. The funeral was corporate but the grave was private. The funeral touched the eternal, but the grave is anchored to the earth. The funeral was... the grave is. We did not linger there, and it was from a distance, some four states removed, that I contributed to the selection of the stone marker and epitaph... seven months ago.

The grave-scar healed quickly as sod took root in the unending Florida summer. Our souls, I have learned, heal at a far slower pace, feeling the passage of each season. My memories have been kind and lively, remembering the joy, the laughter, those moments that belong alone to a father and son. In grief, I have known the rich comfort of friends and family, and a patient understanding not always afforded to those who grieve. It has all gone well, yet it has all seemed, somehow, unfinished. Such were my feelings when I revisited the grave just three days ago, my first visit to his name–my name–our name, etched in stone. It looked as I had expected, polished granite, a rich and muted tone, silk flowers, delivered as promised with Paul's great valedictory in epitaph, "ran the race, kept the faith, finished the course."

Yet, walking away, a piece of the puzzle was still missing, something was incomplete, misinterpreted, lacking in my grasp of sod and granite, of church and grave. I considered what epitaph I might leave one day (if I should leave one at all)... interment or cremation – where I live or where I have lived – what instructions should I leave – how do I make my wishes a matter of record – what should my grave-stone say, (if a grave can speak at all)? And at that moment, Dad's grave spoke! I heard–I knew – I discovered – I decided. Suddenly, it all clicked... his grave, my grave, a tiny piece of ground with marker and message.

Life without my father is buttressed by a steadfast and unshakable hope that I will see him again. For this cause the sting of death is neutralized, and the grave is robbed of victory. The marked location of Dad's grave matters beyond his widow's comfort for this cause: it is that place we can visit, a place marked in perpetuity for one glorious expectation, "from this place the dead shall rise!" I want *that* for my wife, and children, and grands, and greats; for anyone who might find occasion to visit my grave.

I care not for clever words, or a costly stone. It matters not if my body waits under shady trees, on a barren hill, in city or country, shallow sand or heavy loam. Bury me and mark the site with something that shouts louder than my name: "from this place a home-sick soul shall rise." Bury me and let my grave declare the resurrection until that ground is once more broken and there is nothing left of me here, only fully and finally there... in the world to come.

And so, I feel now for my father's grave as I have felt for his victorious passing. I smile–I love–I remember–I rest. I want to visit that place whenever travel takes me near. I want to stand again where he lies just a meter beneath the sod, a body awaiting the trumpet call of God. I want to touch again the stone that marks the life that yet testifies, "As Christ is risen, so too this ransomed soul shall rise." I understand far better now, beyond the intellect to the depths of my emotion, Paul's triumphant query, "O grave, where is your victory?"

Afterword

For sixty-eight years my brother and I became very good at saying "goodbye" to each other. It all started when he felt the call of God and decided I was not qualified enough, at the age of thirteen, to teach him how to become a great preacher so he said "goodbye" and drove sixteen hundred miles west to attend Central Bible Institute in Springfield, Missouri.

Three years after our initial goodbye, he came back home to Bangor, Maine (where I thought he belonged) with his beautiful new bride, Dawn McClure, but three days later he said "goodbye" and proceeded to take off for a twenty-year assignment in Canada.

Through the years, I got my revenge and said "goodbye" to him as often as he did to me. Come to think of it, we never did ask each other's permission.

You would think people who say "goodbye" to each other time and again over sixty-eight years could not possibly have a close, meaningful relationship, but that is where you would be wrong. You see, the fact we had to say "goodbye" a lot made it necessary for us to say "hello" a lot, and when we did it was like we had never been apart.

Together or apart physically, David was my big, brilliant, funny older brother and I always felt close to him. Through the years I have met people who lived in the same house for sixty-eight years but they had nowhere near the close, meaningful relationship enjoyed by my brother and me. Distance is not an insurmountable barrier to love.

Let me tell you about our final "goodbye." I stood apart from the crowd in the middle of the street on March 30, 2014, in Boca Raton, Florida, and watched the back of the hearse, carrying the physical remains of my brother, quite quickly disappear from view. It was there (not the grave) where I said my final "goodbye."

Like many times before he was "hitting the road" but this time it was different. I knew I would never have to say "goodbye" to my brother again.

In just a few days or years, I'm going to see him again. I'll not say "Hey, how ya doin'? " I'll yell "We made it!" and in his ear I'll whisper, "We'll never say 'goodbye' again!"

Charles T. Crabtree
Sacramento, California